Community Support for
Your Path To An EASIER & BETTER Life

Your Path To An EASIER & BETTER Life is an amazing book that will leave you feeling like you can change the world…one "key" at a time. Judy Zerafa has an incredible gift and is able to make complex ideas very simple. This book will leave you inspired.
~*Christine Benero*
President and CEO, Mile High United Way

"I have been in education for 40+ years and I can honestly say I have never found a strategy that made such an impact on students in so many areas of their lives. The Seven Keys to Success explained by Judy Zerafa in her book, *Your Path To An EASIER & BETTER Life,* provide specific, how-to strategies for building positive self-image and achieving and succeeding in school, as well as in all of life. I've heard from many parents about how these strategies have improved their parenting skills and how they can see the improvement in their children's grades and behavior. I use these seven keys with my grandchildren and have seen the positive changes and personal empowerment these strategies have created in them. I highly recommend this book!"
~*Jeannie Courchene*
Principal, 1999-2009, St. Rose of Lima Elementary School, Denver, CO

Many "self help" gurus push complicated agendas for self improvement. Judy Zerafa is not one of them! *Your Path To An EASIER & BETTER Life* transcends jargon, charts a straight forward path for anyone to realize their full potential and, in the process, builds a more civil society. I've seen it in action and it works!
~~*John Arigoni*
President/CEO; Boys & Girls Clubs of Metro Denver

Through her vast experiences, Judy Zerafa has captured straight forward life-changing strategies to engage the minds and hearts of people of every age and walk of life. The message in her book, *Your Path To An EASIER & BETTER Life,* supports every aspect of life in terms of achieving and succeeding. These strategies are the hands-on tools needed by parents who are committed to helping their children become responsible, upstanding adults.
~*Ashley Bright*
Chief Professional Officer; Boys & Girls Clubs of Central Wyoming

As a high school teacher, I have become aware that more and more students are just going through the motions of their lives without goals or the desire to be their best. Many fail to see their lives are determined by day-to-day choices; they can't see that the habits they are developing now will shape their adult lives. Our students need something they are not getting from their parents at home or at school. I recently read *Your Path To An EASIER & BETTER Life*. I believe the strategies of Judy Zerafa's Seven Keys to Success can teach our students, their families and educators the life skills our kids are missing. The message is a common sense approach that can help anyone get on the path to becoming their best.

~*Jack Whitefoot*
Parent and High School Teacher, Las Vegas, NV

What Parents Say About
The Seven Keys to Success Family Programs

The following quotes are from anonymous parent surveys immediately following The Seven Keys to Success Parent Training Programs:

"The most exciting thing I learned tonight was..."

- How using the Seven Keys at school and at home will help my children succeed and be the best they can be!
- How I can use this program for my professional and personal goal setting as well as supporting my children.
- That my children will be taught personal responsibility and how to ensure their own success!
- Tools to be a better parent. Tools to help my son be a better student and happier person. Tools to be a happier self.
- Family goals and how important it is to foster confidence and empower our family.
- That everything I want is within my reach. I can be a wonderful bridge to help my children grow and to help make this world better.
- How to help my children and get beyond a horrible family struggle we are facing.

Additional Comments:

- Thank you for helping us learn these wonderful tools! This information is more valuable than my college education!
- Excellent program! I am so thrilled that my children have been given this opportunity.
- I look forward to "going for it" as a family!

- I am a school counselor and am so excited that my child is part of a school that is using such a wonderful, self-esteem building program!
- Thank you for giving me back my positive attitude and courage to go forward.
- Loved the program. I know it will help my kids and my marriage.
- Since I am in business I am familiar with many of these principles. I am thrilled we are teaching our kids these tools so young. It will make a huge difference in my kids' success.

What Students Say About The GO FOR IT! Seven Keys to Success School Program

The Seven Keys helped me reach my goals. They have helped me have a positive attitude in all of my classes. Key 4 has helped me come early to school. Key 3 helped me do well on my test. This is the best program.
~*Guadalupe, Grade 3*

I used the Seven Keys to change my life by doing better in school. For example, I am doing all my homework now. Also, I'm listening more in school. My mom and I are much happier because I am listening and doing what she says. I'm doing my chores without complaining. These are some of the ways the Seven Keys have changed my life.   ~*Elija, Grade 4*

Mrs. Z has spent 7 wonderful weeks with my school and it's been the best weeks I've ever had. We learned the Seven Keys to Success. Seven Keys is all it takes to a happier and easier life. It not only helps people live life better, but it gives people more self-confidence. They find out that if they believe in themselves, they can believe in everyone else as well.
                                              ~*Vy, Grade 5*

Learning the Seven Keys changed my life because before I started the program, I didn't care about life or school. But since I have had the Seven Keys I don't care what people think about me…I still remember that every day I came to school with a bad attitude because of what happens at my house. Now I wake up and try my best to have the best attitude I can even though my life is hard. The Seven Keys are my life and my salvation.   ~*Areli, Grade 7*

I used to want a lot. I didn't notice all the things I have. I also procrastinated a lot. Then the Seven Keys came along. I try to make more wise choices now and do what I have to do. I have learned to obviously be more positive, to do new things, to build positive habits and make wise choices that will positively affect my future. I have learned to achieve the goals I set for myself and be the person I want to be. I have learned to try and try until I get it...to Go For It! ~Malia, Grade 8

Before I started using Key 2, I was a girl without self confidence and no self-esteem. I was too shy to say what I felt. But now I believe in myself and am even writing my own music! ~Shantel, Grade 8

What Teachers Say About the
Seven Keys to Success Program in the Classroom

Students who understand the Seven Keys to Success recognize and respond to positive attitude in themselves and others. They are less confrontational at school and at home so they come to school with less stress and ready to learn. I witnessed a wonderful transformation of one of my former students when he was in 8th grade. He worked the Seven Keys to Success Program and changed his lackadaisical attitude to that of a totally engaged, more mature, successful student. He wrote two Habit Cards and read them twice every day. Within weeks he had made the honor roll and even became student of the month in middle school. He did this by using those Seven Keys to Success.

~G. A. Prager, Teacher and Reading Specialist, Denver, CO

The Seven Keys to Success School Program was introduced into our district last year. After spending a year using this program in my own life, watching the students incorporate it into their lives, and seeing the interest and effort being put into learning and using this by the parents, I am convinced these Seven Keys to Success are the missing piece in education. The change in mind set, effort and commitment is breathtaking to watch in the results

~Ardyth Fritts, Middle School Teacher, Casper, WY

The message of The Seven Keys to Success by Judy Zerafa is so positively focused and designed to help students, teachers and families in every area of their lives. I can see the changes in how the students see themselves and their lives in a new and empowered way.

~Zach Becker, Third Grade Teacher

As the Librarian in an Elementary School for the past twenty-three years, I know not every student has advanced proficiency in math or reading. Perhaps his or her gift is art or music. The magic of The Seven Keys to Success is that the skills taught help every child uncover strengths and abilities they can develop and through which they can achieve and succeed. These skills are vital to developing confidence, creating healthy relationships and living a fulfilling life at every age. I can see the personal strength and positive attitude I've developed from these keys in my own life. I use them every day.
~*Karen Tower, Librarian, Natrona County School District, WY*

Your Path to An *Easier* & BETTER Life

Based on
The Seven Keys to Success Life Program™
by Judy Zerafa

Your Path To An EASIER & BETTER Life
A How-To Guide For
You & Your Family

Copyright © 2013 by Judy Zerafa, Denver, Colorado. All rights reserved.

No part of this book may be reproduced or transmitted in any form by any means, electronic, mechanical, photocopying, recording, or otherwise, without the prior written permission of the publisher. For information on getting permission for reprints and excerpts, contact the Go For It! Partners.

Printed in the United States of America

First Edition

Published by Go For It! Partners
2500 Cherry Creek South Dr., Suite 110
Denver, CO 80209

ISBN # 978-0-615-84816-7

Book Editor: Paulette Whitcomb, WhitcombWords
Book Design and Composition: Debi Knight, Knight Design Studio
Cover Design: David McMurtry & Judy Zerafa

Notice of Liability The information in this book is distributed on an "As Is" basis, without warranty. While every precaution has been taken in the preparation of the book, neither the author nor the Go For It! Partners shall have any liability to any person or entity with respect to any loss or damage caused or alleged to be caused directly or indirectly by the instructions contained in this book.

DEDICATION
*To the Memory of
Nancy Foreman Fransecky*

My first book, *GO FOR IT!*, was published by Workman Publishing in 1982. The *Washington Post* ran an article about it being the first self-help book ever written for young people. Because of that article, I was invited to be a guest on *The TODAY Show*. The events that unfolded following this interview allowed me to discover my purpose in life. For 28 years, I assumed my appearance on that show had been created by the PR staff at Workman Publishing. I only discovered in July 2011 who was actually responsible for the opportunity that has brought such joy into my life for nearly three decades. Nancy Foreman Fransecky was the Lifestyle Feature Reporter for *The TODAY Show*. She was also a mom who understood how challenging life is for young people. It was Nancy who read the *Post* article and decided to interview me for a February 1983 segment on *The TODAY Show*.

Nancy Foreman Fransecky's wisdom, professionalism and insight provided the springboard from which the *Seven Keys to Success* were discovered. The impact of that interview literally created the opportunity for hundreds of thousands of children to learn to believe in themselves; for parents to learn how to encourage their children and improve their own lives; for teachers to be taught how to provide essential life-skills for their students.

Nancy passed away without knowing what she had made possible for children, families and teachers. I learned of Nancy's passing during the summer of 2011. This book is dedicated to Nancy.

Nancy's husband, Roger Fransecky, established a scholarship in Nancy's memory at the University of Nebraska in Lincoln, where Nancy received her degree in Journalism.

Nancy, I know you are in a place where you know all of this now. I hope what we're doing because of you brings your spirit joy. I pray the young men and women who are awarded the Journalism scholarship in your name grow in their professionalism, integrity and hard work. These were the personal qualities that became the signature for all you accomplished in your life.

IN HONOR OF ALL FAMILIES

Regardless of how "family" is defined,
the family unit has always been the foundation
of any society. It is only through the strength
and determination of the family
that we have the opportunity
to become a great society.

TABLE OF CONTENTS

Introduction: **1**
    The Time for Change Is Now

Before You Begin **9**

Key 1. A Positive Attitude: **13**
    What attitude is and how it works
    How to check and change your attitude

Key 2. Belief in One's Self: **34**
    How to uncover your potential
    How to develop your talents and abilities

Key 3. Positive Habits: **48**
    How habits are formed
    How to replace self-defeating habits

Key 4. Wise Choices: **66**
    Choices as personal power
    How to make choices that bring desired results

Key 5. Setting and Achieving Goals: **80**
    Live your dreams
    How to set and achieve goals

Key 6. Using Creative Imagination: **100**
    How to use the gift of imagination to accelerate
    progress toward goal achievement and personal growth

Key 7. Persistence: **126**
    A deliberate decision to keep trying until
    success is achieved

Continued on next page

An Unforeseen Connection **132**

In Conclusion: **140**
    Now Is the Time to *GO FOR IT!*

Acknowledgements **144**

Appendices

    Appendix A: Dictionary **150**

    Appendix B: Habit Cards **158**

A Positive Attitude • Belief in One's Self • Positive Habits
Wise Choices • Setting and Achieving Goals
Using Creative Imagination • Persistence

INTRODUCTION

The Time for An Easier and Better Life Is Now

If you feel more challenged and frustrated than you believed you would ever feel in your life, you have joined the majority experience of today.

Everywhere you go…friends, relatives, co-workers and neighbors are expressing these same feelings. We're all asking the same questions: Will there be a better tomorrow? Will we have better opportunities in the future? Will our relationships improve? Will we be able to earn enough money to fulfill our obligations? Will our children's challenges tomorrow be even greater than our own today? What happened to the American Dream? **How many times have you wished your life and your loved ones' lives could be easier and better?**

The challenges we are facing – as individuals, families, employers/employees, and as citizens of this country – can be met and significantly overcome. Can we afford to wait for someone to make things better for us? Probably not. It's time to remember what our parents and grandparents told us when we were young: "If you want the job done right, you've got to do it yourself." It's time to dig in and do this job ourselves. We have to start with the basics: **The change we hope to see in our country and around the world must begin within ourselves, within our own families.**

The information in this book will give you the tools to create the change in yourself, and in your family, that will allow you to have the life you hoped you would have, the life you want for those you love. How can I make this promise? Because I've seen the evidence of positive change in my own life. I've listened to employers, teachers, parents and students tell me what they've experienced from using this knowledge. This book explains the principles and strategic steps for personal achievement and success that have been used by some of the most successful people who have ever lived. The principles taught here are those you've heard about all your life. **The difference between The GO FOR IT! Seven Keys to Success and anything you have heard or read before is the precise explanation of each Key and the specific how-to steps for applying this knowledge in your daily life.**

Let me explain how this knowledge came into my life.

When I was a child, no one in my family had ever gone to college. We were poor. I didn't know that at the time; I only knew I was happy. I had wonderful parents and two incredible sisters who loved me. It wasn't until I was graduating from high school that I began to perceive the boundaries created by our family's circumstances. I remember my mother telling me not to dream. She said not having a dream would protect me from getting hurt. My mother told me not to reach beyond where I was standing. No one had ever taught her what it takes to succeed. Because she lacked that knowledge, she was unable to teach me.

I married shortly after high school. By the time I was in my mid-twenties, I was divorced and raising three children on my own in a little town in Northern Michigan, hundreds of miles from my family and friends. Reality sank in as I tried to find a job. With no education, and very little self-confidence, I lived in constant fear of losing my children. This was not the life I had dreamed.

I found a job in the travel industry. One day my employer gave me a ticket to a seminar on self-improvement. That was my first experience with the concept of personal change. I learned two things I was determined to use to better myself and my circumstances. I was excited. I tried to explain what I had learned to my young children.

A few weeks later, the principal at my children's school called to talk with me about their increased academic and personal achievement. She asked what I thought was causing this surprising change. The only thing I could think of was the conversations we were having at dinner. I explained how I was teaching my son and daughters the self-improvement strategies I'd recently learned at a seminar.

Shortly after that call from the principal, I began volunteering my time with elementary students in our community. The success of what I was teaching became the catalyst for a series of miracles that led to my writing the first book on self-help for young people. *GO FOR IT!* was published by Workman Publishing of New York in 1982. After an appearance on *The TODAY Show*, the president of one of GM's divisions called and asked me to teach his executive management team "the secrets to success."

"I think you have me confused with someone else," I told him. "I'm the lady who works with kids."

"I know who you are," he bellowed. "I've read your book from cover to cover and I don't have one person on my executive team who knows how to succeed! I'm asking you to come and teach them!"

I thanked the man from GM, but declined his offer. The next day, someone from Phillips Petroleum called with the same request. Over the next few weeks, there were at least ten calls just like the first two.

It finally dawned on me that the reason children have no idea what it takes to succeed in life is because we, the adults in their lives, aren't sure what it takes either. We stumbled our way through adolescent and teen years into adulthood. Through trial and error, we figured out some things that worked for us, and others that didn't. We tell ourselves and our children, "We're doing the best we can." We encourage our children to do the same.

I *knew* we needed to find a better way! If I was committed to helping children learn to succeed, I would need to begin by providing help and information to adults first. I realized there was more to personal achieving and success than I'd written in my little book. Where would I find all this knowledge? I needed to learn quickly! But how?

> **If I was committed to helping children learn to succeed, I would need to begin by providing help and information to adults first.**

I prayed for guidance.

I remembered how kind the producer at *The TODAY Show* had been when my segment was taped. We bonded. I had her name and phone number somewhere ... I found it, and placed a call to Ronee Hoade at NBC. I explained what had happened as a result of my appearance on her show and told her I needed help.

"I need to know everything there is to know about success," I explained.

Ronee laughed. "How do you think I might help?" she asked.

"You've had the most successful people in the world on your show. I want to interview some of them. I need to find out how they became so successful."

Without a pause, Ronee responded. "I know how to make this happen," she said in her soft spoken, well-modulated tone. "I'll introduce you to Helen Gray. She's executive director of the Horatio Alger Awards."

The Horatio Alger Award is given annually to men and women in our country who have achieved success through their own determination and hard work. I interviewed 35 who had received this distinction, asking only one question: "What do you think you know...that you think nobody else knows ... that has allowed you to succeed to the degree for which you've been honored?"

> **My mind raced as I thought how incredible it would be if everyone had the opportunity to learn all seven keys.**

Everyone was eager to share the story of how he or she had risen to the top. Once the interviews were completed, I reviewed the information I'd gathered. There were seven specific principles to which these successful men and women kept referring. On a legal pad, I identified these as "the keys to success." As I reviewed the information a second time, I realized 30 of those 35 recipients knew only a combination of three of the seven keys. Yet, with an understanding of only three keys, those 30 people had risen to the top of their fields! My mind raced as I thought how incredible it would be if *everyone* had the opportunity to learn all seven keys.

The Seven Keys to Success are:
- A Positive Attitude
- Belief in One's Self
- Positive Habits
- Wise Choices
- Setting and Achieving Goals
- Using Creative Imagination
- Persistence

Nothing on this list is a surprise, is it? When you were growing up, weren't you encouraged to change your attitude? Believe in yourself? Develop positive habits? Make wise choices? Set goals? Be persistent? Your parents urged you to do these. Maybe your grandparents or other relatives did, too. And, your teachers? I'm sure most of them did! But … did anyone ever tell you specifically how to do these things?

All 35 Horatio Alger Award recipients I interviewed told me it is impossible to succeed at anything in life without a positive attitude! When I asked them to explain scientifically what attitude is, how it works, how to determine your attitude at any given moment … and how to change your attitude when it isn't what you need it to be … not one of those 35 people could do so! Each person had an intuitive understanding … based on his or her own life experience … but no one could articulate the specifics of this understanding, or the steps for applying it.

The GO FOR IT! Seven Keys to Success Program is different from any other success or personal improvement program because it teaches the science of each Key. It explains the specific how-tos for applying each Key in the routine of daily life.

The Horatio Alger Award was presented for the first time in 1947. Every year since, multiple recipients have been named. Below is a partial list of some who have inspired me. (To view the entire list, please go to www.HoratioAlger.com.)

Henry Lewis (Hank) Aaron	Sherry Lansing
Buzz Aldrin	Rod McKuen
Philip Anschutz	Thomas Monaghan
Joseph Antonini	Louise Herrington Ornelas

Tom Brokaw	Katherine Ortega
Dorothy L. Brown, M.D.	Colin Powell
(I urge you to read her story!)	Condoleezza Rice
Pearl S. Buck	Tom Selleck
William Dearden	Willlie Shoemaker
(My very first interview!)	Roger Stauback
Lou Dobbs	W. Clement Stone
Julius W. Erving (Dr. J)	Ted Turner
Wayne Gretzky	Denzel Washington
Rick Hendrick III	Oprah Winfrey
Delores Kesler	Chuck Yeager

My experience with the Horatio Alger Award recipients brought with it an understanding of what I wanted to do with the rest of my life. I would translate what I had learned from my interviews with these remarkable men and women into language and strategies that could be understood and practiced by anyone. In that moment, The GO FOR IT! Seven Keys to Success message was born.

This message was born when I realized that, in addition to their belief that a positive attitude is absolutely fundamental to achieving success, the only other thing these accomplished men and women had in common was that each had begun his or her life in an ordinary way. Through their *determination and effort*, however, their lives were transformed into extraordinary examples of accomplishment and success.

My hope and fervent prayer is that YOU come to realize that the opportunity to experience extraordinary success and achievement is fully available to you and your family through your own effort and determination.

The GO FOR IT! Seven Keys to Success was first presented as a school assembly for elementary students. Teachers wanted to know more! They asked me to develop an in-service for them. Students shared the Keys with their parents ... and a workshop for parents evolved. Eventually the GO FOR IT! Program attracted a number of community leaders in Denver, Colorado, who decided to create the GO FOR IT! Institute for the purpose of expanding the message and reaching a greater audience.

In 2007, the GO FOR IT! message became a curriculum offered as master-level Continuing Education Credits for educators who would then teach the Seven Keys in their classrooms. A grant from the Anschutz Foundation provided an "immersion" program at Trevista at Horace Mann, a Denver Public School for grades ECE through the 8th, which trained all their teachers and support staff. A grant from Oprah's Angel Network provided funding to measure the efficacy of this program. Those measurements are detailed following Key 7 in the chapter "An Unforeseen Connection."

A brief mention of the Oprah's Angel Network grant in the *Denver Post* brought requests from around the world asking us to make the message of the Seven Keys to Success available to the public. "We are all looking for a way to make our lives easier... and better," was the comment that made me realize it was time to write this book.

The family has always been – and always will be – the cornerstone of any society. For that reason, I have written this book for families ... knowing we may have different definitions for *family* in our lives today.

Yours may be a traditional family with two fully participating parents. You may be a single parent with custody, shared custody or occasional custody. You may be single ... with the desire to have a family one day. You may be a grandparent or other relative who wants to role-model success for the younger generation in your extended family.

> **The family has always been – and always will be – the cornerstone of any society.**

You may be a minister, an employer, a supervisor, a first-time employee ... or still in school. To you, *family* may represent your congregation, your employees, your co-workers ... or your fellow students.

Whatever role you fulfill in society, *who* you are and *how* you live your life connect you to the reality of today and the hope for tomorrow within the *human family*. The message of the Seven Keys to Success offers you knowledge and strategies for being the person you want to be, and living your life in a way that leaves the world better because you have been here.

Let us know how you are doing along the way. Visit us at www.EasierBetterLife.com or www.facebook.com/EasierBetterLife. If you have questions, we will do our best to answer them. Your comments will help us improve. If you and your family develop activities to support your practice and success with the Seven Keys, please share them with us. Your creativity may be just what another family needs. And … when you experience the positive changes this message can bring, we hope you will tell your friends! The more people who learn to take responsibility for the success of their lives, the greater the opportunity you and your family will have to experience the world as you want it to be.

Thank you for purchasing this book. Your support will allow us to expand our message and reach a wider audience. Our next project will be an on-line platform from which we will provide our continuing education training for teachers around the world. A significant portion of each book sale will be used to develop and launch this platform.

I'm excited for your future. You will be in my thoughts and prayers each day. I believe in you and am cheering your success!

Judy Z

A Positive Attitude • Belief in One's Self • Positive Habits
Wise Choices • Setting and Achieving Goals
Using Creative Imagination • Persistence

BEFORE YOU BEGIN

You will see the text in each chapter is written for the adult in your family who will act as leader of this program. We'll assume it's you. Before you begin the Seven Keys to Success with your family, we strongly encourage you to read the material in advance (or at least the chapter titled Key 1 – A Positive Attitude) to help you decide how, when and where your family sessions will work best.

For pre-K through third-grade children, you may want to explain the core concepts of each Key in your own words. If your children are old enough, you may decide to have them take turns with you in reading parts of each chapter aloud.

The Family Activities at the end of each Key provide the understanding and implementing strategies for all age groups in the family; children not yet in school will need some adult help but they need to be present.

It is important that everyone in your family participate in the Family Activities. If your children are too young to write their answers, help them to verbalize their responses. If you feel it will be helpful, write your child's answers in his or her own notebook. All your notebooks will become valuable as you begin setting and achieving your personal and family goals. Three-year-olds may be too young to concentrate for more than a few minutes at a time, but in our experience, it is always a surprise to see how much they understand and remember!

Personal and family success

Everyone old enough to write will need his or her own spiral notebook and pen. Before your first Seven Keys to Success session, have everyone put his or her name on the notebook. On the first page, have them draw a line from the top of the page to the bottom. On the left side, have each person write his or her definition of "personal success," and on the right side, his or her definition of "family success."

Remind each person in your family that there is no one-size-fits-all definition for success. There are no "right" or "wrong" answers either. What success means to the rest of the world isn't necessarily what it should mean to any of you personally or as a family. Encourage everyone to think of success as a destination, because unless you know where you're going, how will you know if ... or when ... you arrive? If you've never discussed the topic of success with your family before, make sure you give everyone sufficient time to consider his or her definition before you have your first Seven Keys to Success session.

Timelines

There is no timeline for completing the Seven Keys to Success program with your family. Take as much time as you need, or want, with each chapter. Each Key provides a critical piece of knowledge and strategies for making your lives easier and better – as well as for helping you achieve the success you desire. If it's possible, we urge you to spend an hour each week for six months learning, discussing and doing the activity work.

> **Remind each person in your family that there is no one-size-fits-all definition for success.**

When teachers provide this training in their classrooms, they normally take a month to teach Key 1. **The importance of this Key can't be overemphasized. It's the foundation for everything that follows.**

In classrooms, students learn the core concept of each new Key in one day. On a weekly basis thereafter, specific time is devoted to discussion, related stories and activities, all designed to reinforce the understanding and practice of the Key. In between these class training periods, the vocabulary of the Key is reinforced and its use is woven into the daily school routine.

Once you begin this program with your family, you will figure out what works best for all of you in terms of the time you will need or want to spend on learning the concept of each Key, and what works best for reinforcing the practice and activities.

If you see positive changes from the strategies in this book, I hope you will recommend *Your Path To An EASIER & BETTER Life* to your family and friends. Additional sales of this book will make me happy of course, but that is not the reason I'm asking for your help. The reason is this: The more people who understand and use these self-empowering strategies, the less victim mentality, bullying, crime, poverty, promiscuity, etc., we will experience as a society. The opportunity to experience a happier, healthier, more productive, successful life will increase exponentially for us and our loved ones, the more we share the Seven Keys to Success and these strategies.

A Positive Attitude

KEY 1

What Attitude Is

How It Works

How to Check and Change Your Attitude

Fundamentals

- Attitude is mental energy; you are generating this energy every moment you are awake.

- Mental energy (Attitude) is like electrical energy: It's either positive or negative. There is never a time when you can have a neutral attitude. Positive or negative. One or the other. No other option.

- There is a complete match between your attitude and what you attract into your life. Like electrical energy, your mental energy *creates magnetic attraction.* When your attitude is positive, what you pull from others are the positive aspects of their personality or character. When your attitude is positive, you are more likely to get the cooperation of others. When your attitude is negative, you attract the negative aspects of personality or character in those with whom you are interacting. With a negative attitude, it is very difficult to get cooperation from others.

- The same magnetic force applies to what you attract from the opportunities and experiences of your life. When your attitude is positive, you attract opportunities that will move you forward and bring what you desire. With a positive attitude, your experiences will almost always be positive and uplifting. Conversely, when your attitude is negative, the opportunities you draw toward yourself will hold you back and create obstacles. With a negative attitude, your experiences will, most of the time, be disappointing and unsatisfying.

KEY 1

- No one but you can control your attitude. No one can force you to have an attitude you don't want. You alone control that switch: Positive or negative. You are in charge. Your *understanding* that you have control of your attitude, and your *learning* how to keep it positive give you substantial control over the quality and circumstances of your life.

Having a positive attitude is in your best interest. In fact, a positive attitude is the foundation for making your life **easier and better**. Although this seems simple, it takes time and effort to master because we tend to think of ourselves as "right"… and in the case of attitude, that means we tend to see ourselves as generally having a positive attitude. Most people when asked to define their overall attitude will tell you it is positive.

In reality most of us are generating a negative attitude far more frequently than we imagine. In order to begin improving your life and the lives of the members of your family, it is important that you learn how to determine your attitude at any given moment.

How do you determine your attitude?

The process for determining your attitude is very simple. The honest answer to each of the following four questions is all that is required.

What am I thinking?
What am I saying?
What am I doing?
What am I feeling?

You may be surprised when you begin checking up on yourself how often the answers to those questions are not what you thought they would be. In order to develop a positive attitude as a permanent habit in your life, honest answers to these questions are the key. The most significant difference between people who are successful and those who are not … *is attitude*.

Our predominant attitude is, essentially, a habit we've developed.

Your Path To An EASIER & BETTER Life

KEY 1

The easiest way to make sure your attitude is positive the majority of the time is by spending 30 days checking it frequently.

When I first began doing this, I would set a timer at hour intervals. Each time it rang, I would stop whatever I was doing and ask myself these four questions:

What am I thinking?
What am I saying?
What am I doing?
What am I feeling?

In the beginning, I was surprised to see that I was not as positive as I'd always believed myself to be. I thought I expressed myself in a positive way, but the questions about what I was thinking and feeling let me see that while I was saying or doing positive things, I was thinking and feeling negative ones. **It only takes being negative in one of these four areas to determine that your attitude, at that moment, is negative.** You can be smiling, going about your tasks in a productive way, but **if you are thinking a negative thought … or feeling a negative feeling, such as anger, resentment, etc. … the mental energy you are generating is negative.**

Most of us learn (or are conditioned through experience) to smile in particular situations, such as interacting with difficult relatives, co-workers, employers, customers or certain people. We compensate for feeling we *have* to be pleasant by thinking mean thoughts in the hope of getting ourselves through the encounter. Our children learn to do this, too…from watching us. They will grow up and teach their own children to do the same thing.

> **The most significant difference between people who are successful and those who are not … is attitude.**

We think doing this is some way of getting even with the person we don't like. But thinking mean things about someone you don't like, or having negative feelings about them, is never in our best interest. It sabotages us! **We can't hurt other people with our thoughts and feelings. But every negative thought or feeling we ever have**

KEY 1

about someone else is harming us.

The good news is that we have the power to change our attitude to one that is in our best interest. You can quickly switch your attitude from negative to positive.

Once you have learned to identify your attitude, you are ready to start making the switch from negative to positive. This process is just as simple as the one for identifying your attitude. In the beginning, though, it may not be as easy as it is simple. Focusing on identifying your attitude, and then switching it to positive when it needs switching, becomes easier each time you do it. It is the same as doing sit-ups. The first time you try, it usually isn't easy. The more consistent you are with doing sit-ups, the easier that exercise becomes.

Anyone can learn to do this! Doing it with your family makes it easier than doing it on your own.

> **You can change your attitude from negative to positive in a heartbeat by choosing to find the good in some one or some thing.**

How do you change your attitude?

STRATEGY 1

Look for the Good. If your attitude is being challenged by a person, this strategy encourages you to look for something you like or appreciate about the challenger. Instead of allowing your focus to be on thoughts or feelings that are automatically negative, this strategy encourages you to *choose* to look for something about him or her you *do* like or can appreciate, allowing this *good* thing to be your focus or set-point. Your focus can be something as little as liking the tie he is wearing or appreciating her good posture.

This same strategy works in switching your attitude when the cause of your negativity is an experience you are having. Look at what is going on until you find something about it that is positive. Instead of allowing your thoughts to stay focused on what you don't enjoy about the experience you are having, find one thing you can appreciate about it and let your mind focus on that. Let that be your set-point.

KEY 1

We tend to think of personal habits as things we do…or don't do. More than what we do or don't do, the way we *think* creates the most powerful habits in our lives. For example, there are people we like … and others who irritate us. Most of the time, we can't remember how the like or the dislike started, but it has grown into an instinctive reaction that has become a habit. We see someone, or hear his or her voice, and we have an instant reaction. These reactions trigger an attitude. If we like the person, our attitude is positive. If we dislike the person, our attitude is instantly negative.

This same kind of instant reaction is also attached to everyday activities. Some of our daily routines bring us pleasure; others do not. For many of the things we don't enjoy or appreciate we've long since forgotten the why, but we have created a powerful *habit* of being irritated by them. We feel put upon because we have to do them. Those feelings of being irritated trigger a negative attitude.

In this first strategy, we need to consciously look for the good in people as well as the opportunities and experiences of our lives. The beauty of this strategy is that what we look for is almost always what we find! If you are looking forward to something or expecting a good experience, isn't that usually the way it turns out? When you dread something, or just *know* you are going to be disappointed or let down, isn't that usually what happens? If you consider the experiences of your life until now, you'll be able to see for yourself that **what you seek is nearly always what you find. Expectations are the most accurate predictors of future results! And … expectations are always prompted by your attitude.**

You can change your attitude from negative to positive in a heartbeat by choosing to find the good in some one or some thing.

In all of life, opposite aspects are always both present. The Chinese call this the Yin and the Yang. There is no one whose characteristics are 100% positive, just as there is no one completely devoid of any redeeming qualities. In all of us there is good and bad. This is also true of most opportunities and experiences that come into our lives. If you look closely, you are almost certain to find both the good/bad, gain/loss, positive/negative in every person, opportunity and experience in life.

By consciously choosing to look for the good, you will soon begin to experience more of the good. Every second you are focused on the good in some one or some thing, you have your attitude set in the positive position. You are attracting the cooperation of others along with the opportunities and experiences that will contribute to making your life easier and better.

STRATEGY 2

Make a Change. Social research tells us that from the time a human being becomes cognizant (roughly between the ages of 3 and 4), approximately 85% of that person's life experiences are within his or her control. With that in mind, the next time you find yourself unhappy with who you are or what is going on in your life, ask yourself, "Is there anything I can do that will make me happier with who I am, or improve my circumstances?" In other words: *Is the thing causing my attitude to be negative something I can change?*

If there *is* something you can do to make yourself or your life better, JUST DO IT! Strategy 2 encourages you to find the determination, courage and commitment it takes to make you ... or your circumstances ... better. What could possibly give you a greater feeling of personal power than doing what it takes to make yourself the person you want to be? There will be little in your child's life more valuable than *your example* of creating a positive change in you or your circumstances.

STRATEGY 3

Find a Benefit. If 85% of our life experiences are within our control, that means only 15% of what happens to us over a lifetime is beyond our control.

Most of us have experienced examples of having something happen in our lives that we did not want to have happen ... and that we can do nothing to change. Our response to those tragic experiences is anger, grief, disbelief, frustration and other similar feelings. Our attitude gets stuck in the negative position and we may even start to believe our life is over, that nothing good will ever come our way in the future.

How is it even possible to have a positive attitude when tragedy changes our lives? The answer is that it isn't easy. A positive attitude can be reclaimed ... but it takes work.

It may not be possible to maintain a positive attitude immediately after the loss, but the sooner you begin that process, the sooner healing can start. Strategy 3 asks you to look at what has happened in your life – that you don't want, but can't change – until you are able to find one thing you can turn into or perceive as a benefit to yourself. This benefit is a very personal thing. What you are able to perceive as a benefit may not be something another person involved in this tragedy or loss would perceive the same way. For this reason, Strategy 3 is an extremely personal task. Depending on the level or seriousness of the loss, your search for that benefit may take weeks or even months.

There are, of course, different levels of events that happen over which we have no control. First, there is what I call the traffic-light level.

You're in your car on your way to work, an appointment, or taking your child to school. You're short on time ... and you keep being stopped by red lights. You can't do anything about it. You can, however, choose your attitude in this situation.

> **There will be little in your child's life more valuable than your example of creating a positive change in you or your circumstances.**

You can allow yourself to feel anger, frustration, disbelief that you are experiencing such bad luck. Allowing these feelings is a choice for negative attitude. Another choice might be that you use those 30 seconds at each red light to check and make sure you have everything you need for wherever you are headed. Maybe you could use those 30 seconds to think of something for which you are grateful today. You might use those 30 seconds to turn to your child and say, "Hey buddy,

KEY 1

I just want to make sure you know how much I love you!"

There will be traffic-light level events that happen every day. Stuff you don't want to happen, but can't control. If you are doing your attitude check and change regularly, these little events won't throw you into a negative attitude. You will quickly develop a response that keeps your attitude positive.

The traffic lights are one end of the spectrum of things we can't control. At the other end is the life-changing tragedy or loss level. An example would be learning your spouse wants a divorce, being told your job is being cut, or finding out about the death of someone you love. At that level of things-over-which-you-have-no-control, it would be impossible to find a benefit quickly. Finding a benefit to yourself from a loss of this magnitude will take time. You probably won't even be able to start looking for a benefit right away. That's okay. Take the time you need to grieve. Reach for help if you need it. During a time like this, the only thing you may be able to do with your attitude is have faith. Faith is a holding place for positive attitude. Your faith can be in a higher power, in yourself, in a better tomorrow. As long as you have faith in something or someone, your attitude is where it needs to be.

> **Make sure your child understands that having a positive attitude doesn't mean he or she will always feel happy or be able to smile.**

When you are ready to search for a benefit from your loss, you begin moving forward. Once again, you are taking control. The act of searching keeps your attitude positive. It might take a while to find something you are able to accept as a benefit from your loss. However long it takes is however long it takes. Just keep looking.

When you do find a benefit to yourself from the situation you did not want but cannot change, whenever you find your thoughts, words, actions or feelings about the tragedy or loss going into the negative, **focus your attention on the benefit. This focus will keep your attitude positive and move you forward through the grief.**

There are, of course, other levels of events over which we have no control that range between the traffic-light level and the life-changing tragedy or loss level just described. Make sure your child understands that having a positive attitude doesn't mean he or she will always feel happy or be able to smile. During times when something has happened and it isn't possible to smile or feel happy, a positive attitude is achieved by developing the belief that things will get better ... and by looking for the good.

STRATEGY 4

Use a Feeling Switch. Strategies 1 through 3 take time. They are very effective and you want to learn and use all three. *But* ... what happens when you wake up with a positive attitude, jump excitedly from your cozy bed, ready to start your day, then stub your toe as you trip over the cat? And ... discover you're out of coffee? Who has time (or the motivation!) to figure out which of the first three strategies to use? In a nano-second, your attitude takes an instant dive and the day spirals downhill.

It's at this precise time that you will need Strategy 4. We call this one a *Feeling Switch.*

A Feeling Switch is any memory, phrase, image, gratitude, desire, song, movie, *anything* that puts an instant smile on your face. Your Feeling Switch doesn't need to make sense to anyone but you. The only criterion for a Feeling Switch is that it must make you smile (or better yet ... laugh out loud!) whenever you think of it or say it inside your head. (You know ... like repeating a mantra.)

In the instant you genuinely smile or laugh, your attitude switches to positive. Your Feeling Switch is going to become one of your greatest assets. I know dozens of people who have a library of Feeling Switches. When they need a Feeling Switch, they just grab one off their mental shelf and *say it, imagine it, think it.*

I was watching the *OPRAH Show* one afternoon as Oprah explained how she never goes to sleep at night before writing at least six "gratitudes" for the day that is ending. She explained to her audience how it has been proven that the attitude with which you fall asleep is that in which you arise. Studies have proven you get better rest and greater opportunity for healthy cell regeneration during sleep time entered into with a positive attitude. Conversely, going to sleep with a negative attitude diminishes the quality of your rest and impedes the cell regeneration that your body was designed to optimize during the sleep cycle. I decided from that point forward that I would never go to sleep without listing my gratitudes. It made a lot of sense to me that making that list would not only prepare me for a good night's sleep, but it would also put me in the perfect mental place for choosing my Feeling Switch for the next day.

Semper Paratus is how the U. S. Coast Guard says it; *Always Prepared* is what Boy Scouts say. In Latin or English, it means the same … and it is the perfect way to make sure you don't put yourself at risk of sliding into a negative attitude just when you most need your attitude to be positive. Deciding what you will use as your Feeling Switch tomorrow is the perfect way to end today.

There is no way to exaggerate the importance of having a Feeling Switch on standby. Once you get used to using it, you will see for yourself how easy this Strategy 4 keeps your attitude in the positive, making your life easier and better. If your child is still young enough for tucking in bed at night, this is a perfect time to ask what he or she plans to use as a Feeling Switch the next day. Helping your child get into the habit of doing this at a young age will bring positive benefits throughout your child's entire life.

When you examine these four strategies, you can't help but notice that once you've learned to be aware of your attitude, you are able to see how much of your life your attitude *does* influence or control. **You will also understand that you are the one who controls your attitude. No one else has the power to decide what your attitude will be.** If the only thing you take away from this program is this chapter, it can change your life. Keeping your attitude positive will make your life **easier and better**.

The following story has become part of how the GO FOR IT! Institute teaches Key 1. It is a true story and has empowered thousands of children whose families have been challenged by divorce. This story demonstrates how the strategies for changing your attitude from negative to positive work.

THE TOMMY STORY
by Judy Zerafa

KEY 1

The first time I did the GO FOR IT! Program was in Plano, Texas. My audience was 2,500 sixth-grade students in a large auditorium. For 45 minutes, I explained how important it is to have a positive attitude.

At the end of the assembly, the sixth-graders seemed to like what I had said. All but one boy. His name was Tommy. He asked his teacher if he could talk to "Mrs. Z."

When the other students were out of the auditorium, Tommy walked toward where I was standing.

"May I help you," I asked him.

"My teacher said I could talk to you. I just wanted to tell you I think you are a liar ... and I think your program stinks." I could tell by looking at Tommy that he was very angry and meant what he said.

"Just out of curiosity, why do you think I'm a liar?" I asked.

"You think just because you're a grown-up that kids will believe anything you tell them. Well I don't! I know you were lying to us," Tommy replied.

"What do you think I lied about?" I asked.

"The part where you said, 'No matter how bad a situation is, if you look hard enough, you can find something about the situation you can turn into a benefit for yourself.' I know that's not the truth. Some things are so awful you could never find a benefit no matter how hard you try," Tommy answered.

"Can you give me an example of something you think is so awful you could never find a benefit for yourself?" I asked.

"Yeah. Divorce. No matter how hard you try, you could never find any benefit from divorce!"

"How old are you?" I asked him. "And what do you know about divorce?"

KEY 1

"I'm twelve," he answered. "And I know a lot about divorce because my family just got one."

Tommy had been so angry when he started the conversation with me! But now, he just looked sad and confused.

"I'm really sorry you and your family have gone through this," I said softly. "I've gone through a divorce, too, and I know how much it hurts everyone involved. I have a few minutes before I have to leave. Do you want to talk?"

"Not really. I just wish this hadn't happened. Sometimes I feel like it's all my fault. My mom and dad fight all the time. Maybe if I'd been a better kid, they wouldn't have fought so much."

"I'm pretty sure the divorce wasn't your fault, Tommy," I said. "Why don't you tell me about your life? What was it like before your family got divorced?"

Tommy looked down at the floor and shrugged his shoulders. "All the days were pretty much the same," he said. "I have a sister. When we got home from school, there was a rule we had to start our homework while we were waiting for our parents to get home from work. Mom would get home about a half-hour after we did. She would ask us about our day and start dinner. A half-hour later, our dad would get home. He always asked about our day, too. But then … he'd start drinking. He and mom would start fighting. They would yell all during dinner. Then, they'd go into the living room and keep fighting. The only TV set we had was in the living room so we never got to see our favorite shows. Mostly, we'd just go to our rooms and close the doors so we didn't have to hear what they were saying."

"I'm sorry, Tommy. That must have been hard for you and your sister," I said. "But what about now? Do you all still live together?"

"Duh … I said we got a divorce. My dad lives in an apartment. Me, my sister and our mom live in the house."

"So … What's it like now?"

Tommy shook his head, shrugged his shoulders and said,

"Mom still gets home at the same time. We still have the rule about starting our homework as soon as we get home." He paused for a moment and added, "We all eat together and then mom helps with our homework if we need it. After we finish, we all go into the living room and watch TV. Sometimes we talk to our friends on the phone. It's kind of different."

"You're quite an artist, Tommy," I pointed out.

Tommy looked puzzled. "What do you mean?" he asked.

"You've painted a picture with your words!" I answered. Drawing an imaginary frame in the air, I explained, "Using your words you created a very vivid image here of what your life used to be." Then I drew another imaginary frame next to the first one and added, "And here, you've painted a picture of how things are now." Tommy stared at the places I was pointing to, picturing what he had just described.

"Artists sometimes title their work," I told Tommy. "Your word paintings are so real, I'd like you to title them. Can you do that? Let's start with the picture of the way it used to be at your house. Use one word to describe the whole painting."

Without having to think, Tommy blurted out the word. "Violent. That's what I want to call this one," he said as he pointed to the imaginary painting.

> "Using your words you created a very vivid image here of what your life used to be."

"That's a big word, Tommy. Do you know what that word means?" I asked.

"Yep. I know alright! And that's the right word. That's what I want to call my painting."

"Okay then. How about the other one? What do you want to call the other painting?"

Tommy stood quietly and thought for a moment or two. Finally he said, "Quiet. I think I will call this one Quiet."

"That works," I said. "Will you walk over here with me where we can look at both pictures at the same time?" Then I led him

KEY 1

several feet away from where I had drawn the imaginary frames. "Now take a look at both the paintings you've created, Tommy. I want you to forget your mother, your father and your sister as you look at each of the paintings. Thinking only about yourself, tell me which painting describes what is best for you?"

Tommy stood straight and tall. He turned to look at me.

"Quiet. Living where it is quiet is what's best for me," he said.

I looked at my watch. "Wow!" I said. "You are good! We've been talking for only seven minutes. In just seven minutes, you were able to use Strategy 3. You took a situation you can't change ... and you were able to find a benefit to yourself within that thing you don't want and can't change."

Tommy just stared at me. When he spoke, he said, "You aren't as dumb as I thought you were."

I laughed. "Thank you, Tommy. The next time you find yourself feeling angry, sad ... or any of those other negative feelings you have when you think about the divorce, I want you to make your mind focus on the benefit of living where it is quiet now, where there is no fighting. Make your mind hold onto that thought until you can feel your feelings change. Hold onto that thought until you can feel yourself feel better. That's exactly what Strategy 3 is about. You can do this, Tommy. I know you can."

"I'm glad you came to my school," Tommy admitted. "Thanks to you ... now I know this divorce wasn't my fault. It's my old man's fault. I hate his guts. I'm gonna hate him for the rest of my life for causing this."

"I don't blame you for feeling that way. Sounds like your dad is a real loser. I hate him too," I told Tommy.

Tommy was shocked. "You don't even know my dad!" He challenged. "I don't think it's fair for you to say mean things about him!"

"Can you tell me anything good about your dad so I can change my mind?" I asked.

Tommy thought for a minute. "Well," he answered, "I play in a softball league and my dad comes to every single game. My best friend said he wishes his dad would come to even one game."

"Do you have any idea how much love it takes to show up for every single game?" I asked Tommy. "Maybe your dad has a problem with alcohol, but that doesn't mean he's a bad person. In fact, it sounds like he loves you very much and that you are a priority in his life."

Tommy considered my words. "I think my dad really does love me. Maybe I shouldn't hate him. I'm gonna hate my mom! She's the reason my dad drinks so much. My dad says my mom could make anyone drink because she's such a nag."

"I think you're on to something here, Tommy. It sounds like this is probably all your mom's fault and I think we should both hate your mom because she's really the loser," I told him.

Tommy started to get angry at me again. Then he realized I was playing him. "I see what you're doing. You're gonna make me find something good about my mom now, aren't you?"

"You're very smart. That's exactly what I'm doing."

"Let's see," Tommy said as he rubbed his hand against his jaw. "Well, my mom is the one who drives us to all the practices. She's the best cook in the whole school. She lets us have our friends over whenever we ask."

"We are so done here," I said. "Your parents may not love each other, but they certainly love you! And do you realize how smart you are? In less than 15 minutes, you were able to use Strategies 1 and 3 in switching your attitude from negative to positive. What about strategy 2? What is it about the divorce that upsets you the most?"

Tommy didn't need to think about that question! "I hate how my mom and dad always say such mean things about each other," he replied. "I spend weekends with my dad, and from the time I get into his truck after school Friday afternoon till he brings me home Sunday afternoon, all he does is say mean stuff about my mom."

He went on. "And she's just as bad! The only thing she ever wants to talk about is mean stuff about my dad. They never talk to me about anything except how much they hate each other."

At this point, I realized if I didn't leave right then, I would be late for the next school's program. "Tommy, I want you to do something for me," I said as I quickly wrote my name and address on a piece of paper. "I want you to think whether there is anything you might be able to do to make this situation better for yourself. If there is ... I want you to do whatever you can to make it better ... and then write and tell me about it. Will you do that?"

Tommy said he would.

Five and a half weeks later, I was back home in Michigan when I received a letter from Tommy. He had written a five-page letter!

"Dear Mrs. Z, I just had to tell you what happened since you came to my school. You talked at our school on Wednesday. On Friday my dad picked me up after school. As soon as I got into his truck, he started to say something bad about mom. I just looked at him and said, 'Dad, if all you ever want to do is say mean things about mom, I don't want to stay with you on weekends. I know you don't love her any more ... but I do ... And it hurts me to hear you say such mean things about her. If that's all you want to talk about, I'm just going to stay at mom's.'"

> I was able to do something that made things a lot better for me and my sister and I think for my mom and dad, too.

Tommy said his dad just looked at him, but didn't say a word. He put the key in the ignition and started the truck. As they were pulling away from the curb, his dad turned to Tommy and said, "Hey kid, want to go to a basketball game tonight?"

Tommy's letter said he and his dad went to the basketball game on Friday night. On Saturday, they went to a movie and then out for pizza. He wrote, "Mrs. Z, it was so much fun! We had guy-talk all weekend! Dad never said one mean thing about mom!

"I had the most fun I've ever had with my dad," Tommy's letter continued. "On Sunday afternoon, he took me back to mom's. I could hardly wait to tell her how much fun I'd had. I walked into the living room and she was standing there waiting for me with her arms crossed and a crabby look on her face. She started to say something mean about dad. I put my hand up and said, 'Don't do it, mom. Don't wreck the best time I've ever had with dad. I know you don't love him, but I still do. If all you ever want to do is say mean things about him, I think I should just go live with him.'"

Tommy wrote his mom just stood there, not saying a word. He wrote it was like watching a movie in slow motion. Her head fell forward; her shoulders slumped and she began to cry. When she raised her head, he could see her face was wet with tears. She walked slowly toward Tommy, put her arms around him and hugged him for a long time.

"I'm so sorry, Tommy," his mom said. "I can't believe what I've been doing to you and your sister. Your dad and I love you very much. We will always love you and your sister. We just won't ever live together again. But ... I'm going to make you a promise. I promise you that for the rest of my life, I will never say an unkind thing about your father to you and your sister. I give you my word."

Tommy ended his letter by saying, "You were right, Mrs. Z. I was able to do something that made things a lot better for me and my sister and I think for my mom and dad, too. For five weeks nobody has said anything bad about anybody."

Tommy said that every day since the GO FOR IT! Program he checks his thoughts, words, actions and feelings many times throughout the day. If he finds one that is negative, he uses the steps he learned from the GO FOR IT! Program to switch his attitude from negative to positive."

KEY

1

KEY 1

The Tommy Story: Key Connections

Because we do control our attitude, we control the majority of our life circumstances. While a positive attitude is not a guarantee of happiness or success, it is the best path toward reaching both. A negative attitude is the road to challenges and disappointment.

Understanding the power of your attitude and learning to keep it positive the majority of the time will make it easier to acquire and develop the other six Keys. Working together as a family team will make it easier for you to succeed in this effort as individuals.

For the next 30 days, remind yourself to frequently stop what you are doing and ask:

What am I thinking?
What am I saying?
What am I doing?
What am I feeling?

If the answer to any of those questions is negative, you know exactly what to do to change your mind:

Look for the good.
Make a change.
Find a benefit.
Use a Feeling Switch.

FACTS TO REMEMBER

- Your attitude controls, directs or dramatically impacts everything in your life, including your health and well-being, the ease with which you learn, your relationships, and your economic circumstances.
- A person with a positive attitude has more power to lead and influence others than one with a negative attitude.
- Your attitude is entirely up to you.
- All thought creates a chemical reaction in the brain. Positive thoughts

release endorphins that increase health and well-being. Negative thoughts release chemical poisons that reduce health and well-being.
- The average person has between 40,000 and 60,000 thoughts per day.
- Checking your attitude every hour during the day for the next 30 days and switching it to positive when it is negative will create the mental habit of a positive attitude.
- Your attitude is what initializes the Law of Attraction.

Family Activities

We hope you have fun teaching your children the Seven Keys to Success along *Your Path To An EASIER & BETTER Life*. Remember, children learn most readily by example. As a parent, it is your example that is the most powerful in their lives. You can be sure your child is watching and learning from you. The more you work to incorporate the Seven Keys into your own life, the greater the chances that your children will embrace and adopt them into their lives.

Below are some suggestions for family activities that will help demonstrate the processes and strategies discussed in this Key.

The goal of this chapter is for everyone in the family to understand what attitude is, how it works, and how to develop a positive attitude as a permanent habit. As the family session leader, you may decide to explain the concept of this chapter in your own words; or you may read it aloud, word for word.

While a positive attitude is not a guarantee of happiness or success, it is the best path toward reaching both.

Once you have presented the concept, have everyone turn to the first blank sheet in his or her notebook and write the words "Key 1 – Positive Attitude" at the top of the page. Read the following questions, giving everyone plenty of time to write a response. Before mov-

KEY 1

ing on to the next question, take turns reading your answers aloud. Or ... depending on your family dynamic and the number of people involved, you may decide to give the questions at one session, then schedule another session when everyone will be asked to read responses aloud and give each other feedback. As the session leader, be sure to encourage everyone to be respectful and encouraging.

1. In your notebook, write a short description of a time when your attitude was positive. Include the answers to the following questions:
What were you thinking?
What were you saying?
What were you feeling?
What were you doing?

2. Using answers to the same four questions, write a short description of a time when your attitude was negative.
What were you thinking?
What were you saying?
What were you feeling?
What were you doing?

Make it a point every day to catch someone in your family demonstrating a positive attitude and comment on it.

---

3. Explain how you felt when your attitude was positive and how you felt when your attitude was negative. Which feeling did you enjoy more?

4. Go back to your description of the time you had a negative attitude and explain which of the four strategies (Look for the good; Make a change if you can; Find a benefit for yourself; Use a Feeling Switch) you could have used to flip your attitude from negative to positive. In your notebook, write a brief description of what you might have done.

5. Explain what you think your experience would have been if you had used one of those four strategies to change your negative attitude in that situation.

6. To make sure you understand how a Feeling Switch is supposed to work, do this exercise: Sit straight in your chair, place your hands in your lap and your feet firmly on the floor. With your eyes closed, think about a happy experience you have had in the past. It might have been a surprise birthday party, receiving a gift you didn't expect, the first time you held your new puppy. Think of any experience you have had that made you smile! With your eyes still closed, hold that memory for 30 seconds.

7. Take turns sharing your happy memory and how it made you feel to think about it just now. (Leader, make sure everyone has a chance to share.)

8. On a separate page in your notebook, at the top of the page write these words: My Feeling Switch Library.

9. Start your Feeling Switch Library by writing five things that you know would make you smile (or even laugh out loud!) if you thought about them.

Between now and the next time you have An Easier & Better Life session:
- Make it a point every day to catch someone in your family demonstrating a positive attitude and comment on it. This is a great way to keep everyone in the family on track. (Keep thinking of your family as a team!)
- Before going to sleep each night, choose the Feeling Switch you plan to use the following day and write it on a sticky note. Put the note where you will see it first thing in the morning. Share your Feeling Switch with someone in your family. (Team support!)
- When you have dinner together in the evening, or are riding in the car together, talk about how you checked and changed your attitude when it needed changing during the day. (Team training!)

KEY
1

BELIEF IN ONE'S SELF

How to Uncover Your Potential

How to Develop Your Talents and Abilities

KEY 2

Fundamentals

- Everyone has potential.
- Your potential is the unique combination of your personal *talents and abilities*.
- Belief in your self is directly tied to the development of your talents and abilities.
- Talents and abilities are hidden beneath layers of lack-of-knowledge and layers of lack-of-experience.
- Your interest in something is evidence of a talent or ability in that area.

How do you uncover your interests, talents and abilities?

From the moment of birth, we come into this world with incredible, unlimited potential. Our potential is a treasure hidden within us. This treasure is made up of individual talents and abilities. No two people have the exact same combination; within a family, there may be parents, children, or siblings, who share one or more similar talents or abilities, but each of these family members will not necessarily share others. It is the combination of our talents and abilities that makes us unique. No one has a personal treasure identical to our own.

The talents and abilities within us are hidden beneath layers of lack-of-knowledge and other layers of lack-of-experience. The process for uncovering talents and abilities requires the use of two shovels. One hangs from a hook marked EDUCATION; the other from a hook marked PARTICIPATION. In other words, LEARNING and DOING.

EDUCATION:
Learning something new removes one layer of lack-of-knowledge.

PARTICIPATION:
Doing something new removes one layer of lack-of-experience.

Every time we take the opportunity – whether at school, home or in the community – to learn something new, we are using the shovel marked EDUCATION (or Learning) and removing one layer of lack-of-knowledge. Along the path of learning, we will discover subjects in which we have an interest.

When we take the opportunity to participate in a worthy activity, we are using the other shovel, marked PARTICIPATION (or Doing) and removing one layer of lack-of-experience. Along the way, we will find activities in which we have an interest.

Any interest in a subject or an activity is evidence that a talent or ability has been discovered.

Children may express an interest in a subject, but when they don't get a high mark on their report card in that class, they believe they have no talent in that area. The same is true when they are interested in a particular activity, but don't quickly become "one of the best" in that activity peer group. Our talents and abilities are much like diamonds when they are first discovered. The most valuable diamond in the world looks like a piece of coal when it comes out of the ground. Its full value is only seen after it has been cut and polished. Time and effort are what polish a human talent or ability. *We* have to invest *our* time and *our* effort into developing the value of our talents and abilities.

As a parent, you are in the perfect position to watch for those

> **We have to invest *our* time and *our* effort into developing the value of our talents and abilities.**

KEY 2

sparks of interest and bring them to your son's or daughter's attention. Actually, you are in a great position to do that with anyone with whom you have a relationship. Who knows? You may become someone's Pygmalion!

Uncovering the talents and abilities that make up our potential is not complicated. Anyone can do it. Learning and doing allow any one, of any age, to uncover his or her treasure.

Being able to share in the discovery and development of your child's potential is one of the great joys of being a parent. (This knowledge may also help you stay awake and keep smiling while you drive your son or daughter to all those practices. Just remember … turning the piece of coal into a diamond!)

Below is a poignant example of why this key is particularly important.

When I work with students in the classroom, I always ask how many of their parents dislike going to work. Sadly, too many children raise their hands in response to this question. Then I ask how many of those who raised their hands want to grow up and be like their parents. Jaws and shoulders drop. Eyes get sad. These children say they don't want to grow up and be unhappy.

> **Being able to share in the discovery and development of your child's potential is one of the great joys of being a parent.**

Teaching your child Key 2 will give him or her a chance to find joy and purpose while in school, and later in a job or career connected to one of his or her talents or abilities. This story gives a perfect example of how using Key 2 can make this happen.

BILL THE FISHERMAN STORY
by Judy Zerafa

When I lived in Michigan, I was invited to talk with graduating seniors from a high school in a small village on Lake Michigan. It was the last hour of the school day on a hot Friday afternoon late in May. There were only 22 graduating seniors, and none was paying attention. I kept looking at the clock, willing the time to go by faster. When there were only two minutes left before the bell was to ring, I asked the class how many were going on to further education. Five students raised their hands.

There was one particular boy who had been irritating me for the entire hour. He sat directly in front of where I was standing and had not looked at me once during that hour. I mentally set a goal of having eye contact with him before the day ended. When he didn't raise his hand after I asked the question about going on to college, I moved directly in front of his desk. I stood quietly and stared at him until he looked up. Smiling, I asked, "Is your family wealthy?"

The whole class laughed and let me know nobody in that class was rich. Several called out, "We're all poor."

I kept staring at the boy in front of me. "Does that mean you are going to get a job after you graduate?" The boy shrugged his shoulders and mumbled, "I guess."

"What kind of a job are you looking for?" I asked.

Again, the boy shrugged his shoulders and muttered, "I dunno."

Leaning in closer to the desk, I continued to question the boy. "Well, what do you enjoy doing?"

With that, the boy half-smiled and said, "I love to fish. I've loved fishing all my life."

"Great!" I said. "Look for a job that has something to do with fishing!" With that, the bell rang and the students nearly trampled me on their rush out the door.

I felt that hour with those students had been a waste of time for everyone. Only a rookie would have agreed to a last-hour gig on a Friday afternoon a week before graduation. What was I thinking when I accepted that invitation!!! I left that school as fast as I could and had put the experience out of my mind before I arrived home.

Eight years passed. I was at the Detroit airport one autumn day waiting to board a plane. For the first time in my life, I heard my name paged over the intercom. While walking toward the courtesy phone, I noticed a woman watching me in a curious way. I answered the call and then returned to my seat. As I sat down, the woman who had been watching me rushed over. In an excited voice, she asked, "Are you the Judy Zerafa who works with kids?"

I said that I was.

The woman introduced herself as Mary. She asked me if I remembered talking with a class of seniors in Suttons Bay, Michigan, eight years ago.

I said I didn't remember that particular one, but added that I was invited to a lot of schools and might just have forgotten that one because it had been so many years ago.

Mary explained, "My son, Bill, was in that class. You asked him that day if he was going on to college.. He told you he wasn't. You asked if he planned to get a job. He said he was, but didn't have any ideas of where he would look. You asked what he enjoyed doing and he told you he liked to fish. You suggested he get a job that had something to do with fishing."

The memory of that experience, while still vague, began to surface.

Mary continued: "When Bill came home that afternoon, he told me what you had said. He thought your suggestion was a good idea. The next day he applied for a job at a bait store on the main road that runs along the bay. He was very excited when he learned he had been hired."

When Mary described where Bill had gone to work, I knew exactly where that bait shop was. When I'd lived in Michigan, I'd driven along that road many times each week. "I know right where you mean!" I enthusiastically told Mary. "How interesting! Does he like working there?"

Mary laughed. "He sure did! But he hasn't been there for years. If you have time, I have a story to tell you," she added.

"My plane is delayed. I have all the time you need," I said.

We got comfortable and Mary continued. "Bill loved that job! He would come home from work every evening with stories to tell about the day. He changed so much that summer. He seemed happy all the time. We had a rule in our family that we would have dinner together every day. Bill never said much at the table. In fact, in high school, Bill had become an introvert. The only time I would see him excited was when he and his dad went fishing. Bill would rather fish than do anything.

"When fall came that year, Bill told me he thought he might try to get a job up the road at a company that chartered fishing boats." Mary explained where the charter boat company was located and I couldn't believe the coincidence.

"Oh my gosh!" I said. "I know that company! I know one of the owners! What a coincidence!"

> "You asked what he enjoyed doing and he told you he liked to fish. You suggested he get a job that had something to do with fishing."

"You haven't heard anything yet," Mary assured me. "Wait till I tell you what happened next."

Mary's eyes sparkled with happiness and excitement. I was enjoying this conversation very much. Mary explained that Bill was hired by the charter boat company and everyone there thought he did a great job. Because Bill and his dad had fished the bay for so many years, Bill was able to tell his customers exactly where to go and what bait was best to use for the fish they wanted to catch. Bill's customers began to call ahead and ask for him personally. Mary said Bill always came home with handsome tips from his satisfied customers.

She explained that Bill's personality and self-confidence had dramatically upgraded. He joined his family for dinner as often as he could and regaled them with stories about his customers, the company and, of course, grand tales of big fish. He smiled all the time and took greater interest in his appearance. Bill opened a savings account, and before long had enough money saved to buy a nearly new car.

At the end of the following summer, Bill started talking about moving on and looking for a bigger opportunity. He decided he'd like to work for the company that manufactured the boats he and his dad had used for years, the same boats he'd been chartering for the past 12 months. Mary explained this manufacturing company was several hundred miles from where Bill had lived his whole life. While she was excited by her son's enthusiasm and motivation, she knew she and Bill's dad would miss him very much.

> **She explained that Bill's personality and self-confidence had dramatically upgraded.**

Bill made the move and was hired by the boat manufacturer as an assembly-line worker. For eight hours a day, he bolted seats into the boat hulls. One Friday afternoon, as his shift was coming to a close, Bill became aware someone was standing behind him. He turned – and as he later told his mother – he was staring into the eyes of a giant of a man. Bill said it was the owner of the company and that he looked like a great big bear.

In a gruff voice, the bear-of-a-man asked Bill, "Hey! Are you the kid who keeps stuffing my suggestion box with ideas?"

"Y-yes, sir," Bill stammered.

The big-bear-of-a-man stood silently for a moment, appraising Bill. "Okay then," he said, shaking his head. "Keep putting your suggestions in the box. You've got good ideas. We're gonna use some of 'em."

With that, the big man turned and began walking across the manufacturing floor. Halfway across, he stopped, turned, and walked back toward Bill. "No one knows this yet," the big man said, "but in a couple of weeks, we're gonna hire a new line supervisor. I want you to apply for that job. Fill out the paperwork before you go today, kid."

Bill told his mom that his heart was pounding so fast, all he could do was look at the company owner and nod yes.

Once again, the big man turned and began walking away. But he stopped and turned back again. "You've got a college degree, don't you, kid?"

Bill felt his heart drop to his feet. He shook his head and quietly answered, "No, sir. I didn't go to college."

After another moment, the big man shook his head and said, "Well, then. That's too bad. We only hire college grads for the supervisor positions. Too bad. You probably would have done a good job." With that he turned and walked toward the door.

Bill told his mom that he didn't stop to think. He just ran after the boss. When he caught up with him, he said, "Sir, please give me a chance! I could be a very good supervisor! I know everything about your boats. If you give me a chance, I won't let you down. I'll take classes at night. I can go to college at night. Please. Give me this chance; you won't be sorry."

The big man looked down at Bill for a long time. Finally, he said, "Let me think about it. We've never done this before."

Bill told his mother the boss finally came to see him the following week.

"Here's what we're gonna do, kid. We're gonna give you a trial. You will start as a supervisor in two weeks. In the meantime, you get yourself enrolled in classes. I want to see all your grades and they better be good. You flunk anything and you answer to me, got it?"

KEY
2

Mary said Bill enrolled in college and signed up for classes that very day. She said it took him six years to graduate, but graduate he did. All the time he was attending classes, he worked equally hard at being the best supervisor the boat company ever had. The day of graduation, the big man was there, sitting right in the front row; Mary said when Bill walked across the stage to accept his degree, she saw him wipe away tears.

Two days later, Bill was called into the big man's office. "Close the door," he said. The two men sat across the desk from one another. "I'm really proud of you, Bill. I've never had an employee who worked harder. Or, loved this company more. If I'd ever had a son, I would have wanted him to be just like you."

Bill told his mother that comment made him feel like a giant. The big man continued: "I got some bad news last week. My doctor says I'm not going to be around much longer. I never had kids. I worked hard all my life, and I have no children or relatives to pass this company on to."

I was listening to Mary's story with riveted interest. I watched as tears gathered in her eyes and heard a catch in her voice. I put one arm around her in a hug. She blinked back the tears and continued.

"Bill called me that afternoon to tell me what had happened. This wonderful, kind man who is such a role-model to my son told him he had decided to leave his company to Bill. When I heard your name being paged and watched you walk to that phone, I just had to tell you what happened to my son after you talked to him that day. I wanted to tell you Bill is the happiest person I've ever known because you told him to find a job related to something he enjoyed. I hope you tell all the children how important it is to follow what they love."

Bill the Fisherman Story: Key Connections

I've thought many times since that conversation with Bill's mother about the people I know who have jobs or careers in areas in which they have a strong interest. They are happier, more successful and have more energy than people with no personal interest in what they do. **Those who earn an income by doing something related to a personal interest don't experience their jobs as a necessary evil or drudgery. People who have a talent or ability associated with how they earn a living experience fulfillment and even joy.** This is what we all want for our children, and it is why Key 2 is so important.

And, by the way ... it isn't too late for you to point yourself in the direction of something you enjoy! Perhaps your interests won't result in a new job or career direction, but will be something you do for a hobby. Doing something you enjoy, whether it's for pay or simply for personal enjoyment, gives you a sense of fulfillment. If you are a person of faith, you understand that developing your talents and abilities is a way of serving God.

Make this a family project! Have all family members create a list of the subjects and activities they enjoy. Find a place (the refrigerator?) to post these lists where everyone will see them frequently. Encourage family members to pay attention to what they are learning and the opportunities for trying something new. Keep your lists updated. And ... catch each other being interested! Every time anyone in the family discovers a subject he or she enjoys, or an activity of interest, make sure that is added to the treasure list. Help younger children stay in the game by drawing a picture of what they are interested in learning or doing ... or you can add to their list for them.

> **Encourage family members to pay attention to what they are learning and the opportunities for trying something new.**

These lists may become so long it might not be possible to work on developing everything at once. That's okay! Just keep the lists going, and decide which subjects or activities get extra time and effort now.

KEY 2

As time permits, effort in other areas can be added. The main thing is to never stop learning and doing new things.

When students create a treasure list, it initiates an understanding that they do have personal worth. The addition of new interests increases that understanding. Once your child sees he or she has specific talents and abilities, it is important for you to work together to decide the best way to develop what your child has uncovered. If your child is young, and team practice or lessons are involved, you will be the one who provides the opportunity for exploring and developing these talents or abilities. As your family learns and practices the rest of the Seven Keys to Success, your child will learn how to take responsibility for his or her part in developing these gifts.

If there are grandparents or other older relatives living with you or close by, invite them to be part of your family sessions. Their participation will let your children see that the discovery and development of talents and abilities are possible at every stage of life.

Key 1 teaches us how to have a positive attitude. **Having a positive attitude makes the discovery of new interests and the development of talents and abilities easier to accomplish.** As you learn and use each of the Seven Keys to Success, you will understand how each Key is expanded and made more meaningful by the previous ones. Key 7 connects back to Key 1 and the seven form a circle. Within that circle, your child will have the knowledge and strategies necessary to achieve and succeed academically, personally and, later in life, economically.

Belief in your self is directly tied to the development of your talents and abilities.

FACTS TO REMEMBER

- Everyone has potential.

- Our potential is that unique combination of our personal talents and abilities.

- Talents and abilities are hidden beneath layers of lack-of-knowledge and lack-of-experience.
- Learning something new removes one layer of lack-of-knowledge.
- Doing something new removes one layer of lack-of-experience.
- An interest in something is evidence of talent or ability in that area.
- Belief in your self is directly tied to the development of your talents and abilities.
- A positive attitude opens our minds to the discovery of new interests and the development of talents and abilities throughout our life.

Family Activities

We hope you have fun teaching your children the GO FOR IT! Seven Keys to Success along *Your Path To An EASIER & BETTER Life*. Remember, children learn most readily by example. As a parent, your example is the most powerful example in their lives. You can be sure your child is watching and learning. The more you work to incorporate the Seven Keys into your life, the greater the chances are that your children will embrace and adopt them into their lives.

Below are suggestions for family activities that will help demonstrate the processes and strategies discussed in this Key.

1. Have each family member open his or her spiral notebook and at the top of the next clean page write "Key 2 – Activities." Beneath that heading, ask everyone to draw a line down the middle of the page from top to bottom. On the left side of the page, have everyone write "Subjects I'm Interested In," and on the right side, "Activities I Enjoy."

Have each person make a list of all the subjects and activities in which he or she has an interest or enjoys. Explain that this is an exercise that should continue for the rest of their lives. It's okay if they don't get everything on the list today, but they should remember to add subjects and activities as they remember or discover them. (If your child is too young to write, you can make a list of the subjects and activities in which you've seen that child show interest.) Give everyone five to ten minutes to do this exercise, and then take turns sharing what is on the lists.

2. Once each family member has shared his and her list, give each an opportunity to identify a talent or ability someone else has overlooked.

3. Have each family member copy his and her list of subjects and activities on a separate piece of paper. Ask them to put their name at the top of the page and put their list on the refrigerator or other place where it will be seen regularly. Ask each person to be sure and add any new subject or activity to the list.

4. Over the next week, ask each family member (helping children who aren't old enough) to create a collage of images representing subjects and abilities in which each has an interest. This is a great opportunity for creativity!

> As a family, each month plan one activity or explore one subject together that will be new for at least one member of the family.

5. An alternative to the individual collage would be to do one as a family. In this version, you will be working to create a masterpiece of images that are important and of interest to all of you as a family team.

6. The family collage could develop into a family tradition! Choose a special date and make that the annual Family Collage Day. It will be fun to see how your family interests expand over the years.

7. As a family, each month plan one activity or explore one subject together that will be new for at least one member of the family.

Depending on the age of the children, let each person have a turn at making a suggestion and planning the experience.

8. Between these outings have all family members share thoughts and feelings about the Learning and Doing experience.

KEY 2

POSITIVE HABITS

How Habits Are Formed

How to Replace Self-Defeating Habits

KEY 3

Fundamentals

- Habits run our lives.
- We all have developed habits that are positive (life-enhancing) and others that are negative (self-defeating).
- All habits, whether positive or negative, are developed the same way.

How are habits formed?

All habits are developed in one of three ways:

1. From the time we are old enough to think, every thought we ever have about our self is processed as words by our conscious mind. These words are then sent on electronic impulse to our subconscious mind, where they are translated into an image. This image is then permanently stored in the subconscious part of our mind.

Each time we have a similar thought about our self, our conscious mind sends those words back to our subconscious mind. Once again, the subconscious mind translates these words into an image and stores that image on top of the original one. This layering process creates a three-dimensional representation that is more detailed and vivid than the original image. The more similar thoughts we have about our self, the more layers are added to the image and the more detailed and vivid it continues to become.

2. The same process occurs each time we have a feeling about our self. Our emotions are felt in our solar plexus – that's where we get the term *gut feelings* – then pushed up through our conscious mind and forwarded on electronic impulse to our subconscious. These feelings about our selves are translated into an image and permanently stored. The next time we experience a feeling about our self, identical to one we've had before, that feeling is processed and translated in exactly the same way. This image is stored as a layer on top of the original. The more we experience that same feeling, the more layers we add to the original image, and the more vivid and detailed that image becomes.

3. The third and final way in which habits are formed is through our acceptance of what others say about us. When someone says something about us that we believe is true, whether it is or not, that person's perception is accepted by our conscious mind, sent on electronic impulse to our subconscious mind, then translated into an image and permanently stored. Just like all the identical thoughts and feelings we have about our selves, all identical perceptions of us by other people are processed in the same way and stored in layers on top of the original. The more layers, the more vivid and detailed these images become.

> **These feelings about our selves are translated into an image and permanently stored.**

The primary responsibility of our subconscious mind is to make sure we act in accordance with the images it has stored. The images with the most layers are the ones on which our subconscious mind focuses its greatest attention and effort.

Another important fact about our subconscious mind: It has no power to judge. The effort our subconscious mind puts into making sure our actions are consistent with our subconscious images is free from judgment as to whether what it is pushing us to do is moving us forward or holding us back – helping us, or hurting us.

If we have a highly developed many-layered image – habit – of working out regularly, that drives a lot of our choices during the day.

KEY 3

If we have a habit of watching every penny, that drives many of our decisions, too. Ask your friends what they think runs their lives. They will tell you it's their jobs, their spouses, their finances, their beliefs, their children's practices! But consider both the physical and mental habits that you and your friends have developed over the years. See if you don't agree these have significant control over your daily life.

All of us have habits that move us forward; these are also known as *good* habits. We all have habits that hold us back, aka *bad* habits. Collectively, these are what run our lives.

Our habits – those multi-layered subconscious images – are providing *examples* from which our children are learning. Later in this chapter, you will learn a powerful strategy for erasing habits that are holding you back, and replacing them with habits that will move you forward. Before that point, however, it's important that we consider the power we have with *our words* to influence the development of our children's subconscious images…hence the development of *their* habits.

Most of what younger children think and feel about their selves is triggered by what we say to them as parents. As our children get older, their thinking becomes more independent, but even so, we continue to have substantial influence on what our children think and feel about their selves throughout their lives. What we say, and how we say it, provide daily opportunities for our sons and daughters to develop subconscious images, many of which will become life-long behavior patterns. **The more effort we put into having a positive attitude (Key 1) when interacting with our children, the better the chances that our words and body language will prompt them to thoughts and feelings about their selves that will create positive subconscious images.**

> **You will learn a powerful strategy for erasing habits that are holding you back, and replacing them with habits that will move you forward.**

Catching your child behaving in a positive way, and favorably commenting on it, are powerful reinforcements for creating positive subconscious images. Catching and commenting negatively on inappropriate behaviors are equally powerful in reinforcing negative images … *if that is where the communication ends.* When you see or learn your child is behaving in a misguided or unsuitable way, help him or her understand that these actions are opposed to who you think he or she is. For example: You see your son or daughter taking away a toy another child is playing with. Rather than raise your voice and embarrass or upset your child, you take him or her aside and say something like, "What you just did surprised me. You have such a kind heart. Taking away someone else's toy isn't like you!" Ask your child to explain what happened, and tell you what he or she thinks would be a better plan if the same situation came up in the future. When you feel comfortable with your child's explanation, let the child see and hear your pride in his or her ability to behave well, do the right thing, and learn to do the right thing in the future.

Fundamentals

- The subconscious mind has more power than the conscious mind.
- The subconscious mind works primarily with images.
- The subconscious mind has no power to judge.
- The primary responsibility of the subconscious is to make sure we act in accordance with the images of our selves stored in that part of our mind.
- The greater the number of overlays to any subconscious image, the more effort is applied to matching our behavior to the corresponding image.

In 2006, Bruce Lipton, Ph.D., wrote *The Biology of Belief*, in which he explains that the subconscious mind has nearly one million times the power of the conscious mind. Dr. Lipton's work is so groundbreaking and important that he received the USA Book News' 2006 Award for Best Book in Science. Because of what we now know about the power of the subconscious mind, understanding Key 3 is of critical importance. One of the most valuable statements in this Key is:

When a person tries consciously to go against a well-developed subconscious image, there is little chance of success.

The habit of being overweight is a perfect example of how the subconscious mind works. We all know people who've gone on a particular diet. They stick to the rules of whatever diet they're on, and they lose weight. Before long, however, you see them regaining the weight they've lost. Without a doubt, these people are carrying around highly layered images of themselves as overweight. They are able to consciously override this subconscious image for a period of time. Ultimately, the subconscious takes control, and they move back into the behaviors that are consistent with their image of being overweight. **The subconscious mind is responsible for guarding and perpetuating the layered image of** *I am overweight* **and does what it has to do to keep the image true ... including making us feel hungry or crave foods. It even controls and adjusts our metabolism.**

The good news is that *any* self-defeating habit can be replaced with one that is life-enhancing. We *can* replace life-long habits that keep us from being who we want to be.

Fundamentals

Positive habits:

- make our lives easier.
- make our lives better.
- can be created to erase and replace self-defeating habits.
- earn the respect of others.
- provide positive examples from which others may learn.
- make it easier to reach our goals.
- give us an increased level of confidence and self-esteem.

What is the process for replacing self-defeating habits with positive habits?

The process for removing a self-defeating habit is very simple. The first step is to identify the habit keeping you from being, or having, what you desire. Once you have identified the behavior you want to remove, you write a clear description of the way you want to be in this area of your life.

Take as much time as you need to be sure you are clear about how you want to act, feel and be perceived by your self and others. Once you are clear, pare down what you've written to no more than two very enthusiastic, first-person, present-tense sentences. Copy those sentences onto a 3x5 card. You have just created a HABIT CARD!

A HABIT CARD is a simple, highly effective method for removing a negative, self-defeating image and replacing it with a positive, life-enhancing one.

HABIT CARDS also work when there isn't a negative image holding you back, but you want to create a new, life-enhancing behavior. You add a new habit just like you undo a negative one. Write a very clear description of how you want to act, feel and be perceived by your self and others in a specific situation or within a particular life issue. Once you have clarity, distill what you have written into no more than two enthusiastic, first-person, present-tense sentences and copy them onto a 3x5 card.

KEY **3**

> **Take as much time as you need to be sure you are clear about how you want to act, feel and be perceived by your self and others.**

What are the rules for effectively creating a HABIT CARD?

A HABIT CARD always starts with the word *I* and is followed by your *first and last names*. The fourth word must be one of these three: *am – only – always*. Or by a combination: *am only – am always*. What follows will create an effective HABIT CARD.

When you say the word *I*, your subconscious mind comes to immediate attention because you are talking about your self … and your subconscious is there to serve *you*. With the word *I*, you get its attention. It has a clear image of *I*. When you follow the word *I* with your first and last names, you have removed any doubt this is going to be all about *you*.

That fourth word, *am*, is the most powerful word in any language. The word *am* turns on the power of the universe. The word *am* means *what-is-so*.

I first got a glimpse of what runs our lives when I attended a motivational seminar over 25 years ago. The trainer asked if anyone in the room had a habit he or she wanted to change. I was not as outgoing then as I am today, so I shocked myself by raising not just one hand, but both. I wanted to make sure the trainer called on me! My habit of always being late was negatively impacting every aspect of my life. The day before that seminar, three incidents caused by this habit had piled one on top of the other…and I knew I had to find a way to get rid of it.

The previous morning, as I drove my three children to school, none of them would talk to me. Everyone was mad at mommy. All three were going to have to stay after school that day because they had been late for class every day that week. The principal couldn't make me stay after school … but she could punish my children. Everyone involved knew I was the one who caused my two daughters and son to be late. I didn't get a hug goodbye that day!

> That fourth word, *am*, is the most powerful word in any language. The word *am* turns on the power of the universe.

When I arrived at work, my boss was standing outside my cubicle. He said, "Judy, you are a hard worker and everyone likes you … but you're late for work every single day. I can't let this continue because it sends a message that I'm okay with people coming in late. Starting this pay period, you will be docked for each minute you are late."

"Great!" I thought. I was a single mom who struggled every day to make ends meet. I couldn't afford to lose a penny of my pay! "What a lousy start to the day," I said under my breath. The good news was that I had something I was looking forward to that evening. I would concentrate on that and forget how the day had started.

I'd been dating someone for several months. He was smart, funny, successful and considered a real catch. I looked forward to that evening and put aside all thoughts of the morning.

I picked my children up at school and, once again, we drove in silence. I fixed their favorite dinner and explained to the sitter what they could do and how late they could stay up. I put on a different outfit, fixed my hair and makeup, then headed back into town where my date and I had agreed to meet. When I arrived at the restaurant, McDreamy was already seated. He stood as I walked toward our table … but he wasn't smiling. Once I was seated, he looked at me and said, "Judy, you are a very nice person and I've enjoyed getting to know you … but this isn't going to work for me. We've been dating for three months and you've not been on time for anything since we met."

Oh my gosh! He was breaking up with me! "But you know I have children," I explained. "It's very hard to be on time when you have three little kids!" I argued.

"I hear what you're saying," he replied. "But what about the weekends when you don't have your children? Or the times we've met for lunch during the week? Your children aren't the issue then. But you're still always late."

He went on to explain. "Time is a big issue to me. I was raised to believe that being on time is an act of respect to others. I don't feel you respect me when you make me wait for you every single time. I want us to enjoy our dinner this evening, but I have to be honest and tell you I won't be asking you out again."

Now you understand why I waved both hands in the air the next day when the trainer asked if there was anyone who had a seriously unwanted habit.

When I explained what had happened the day before, the trainer asked the rest of the audience if anyone else had a problem with being on time. About a third of the people raised their hands. And then, the focus was back on me.

"How long have you had this habit?" he asked.

I explained that my being late was the only thing I remembered my father ever yelling about when I was growing up. I made my family late for church regularly. My mother had to drive me to school more

KEY

3

than once because I had missed the bus. When I was older, there were so many times when friends would be upset with me because we'd missed the start of a football game or movie.

The trainer asked if I could remember thinking about the fact that I was late so often.

"Vividly," I answered.

"Did you ever have feelings related to your being late?" he asked.

"Constantly."

"And ... did people tell you that you were someone who was always late?"

"Every single day. And, I knew they were telling the truth."

The next thing the trainer wanted to know was if I ever consciously tried to be on time and what strategies I used in my attempts.

Everyone with the habit of being late laughed and nodded in agreement as I explained my failed attempts for getting to school and work on time in the morning ... set the clock 20 minutes ahead to trick myself ... pack lunches and lay out what I was going to wear the next day before going to bed ... and ... so ... on ...! I would be ready to walk out the door 10 minutes ahead of time and something would always happen! I couldn't find the car keys ... I remembered I had to pick up one of my children's classmates ... always something.

When everyone stopped laughing, the trainer explained how to get rid of an unwanted habit. First, we were told to identify and describe the habit. Next, he explained, we were to write a description of the way we wanted to be.

The whole idea seemed beyond lame to me! I could hear the people sitting near me muttering under their breath about not believing it would work either. Someone asked the trainer how anything that simple could get rid of a rotten habit he had had for years.

"I can't really explain how it works," the trainer answered. "I just know it does. If you're serious about getting rid of a habit you don't want, this will do the job. It's okay with me if you don't believe what I'm telling you. Just try it and see for yourselves."

I was desperate. I decided to give the strategy a try, as nothing I'd done before had worked.

The trainer asked us to start the process by writing several paragraphs explaining how we wanted to be in contrast to the unwanted habit that was holding us back. I wrote as fast as I could about how I wanted to be someone who was always on time. Someone people could count on.

Next, we were to boil down what we'd written into no more than two statements expressing exactly how we wanted to act, be, and be regarded by others. I wrote on the seminar pad: "My name is Judy Zerafa and *I am never late!*"

The trainer asked me to read what I'd written. I read it with enthusiasm.

"Okay," the trainer said. "Let me explain how this is going to work." And he outlined a scenario where the word *I* played a crucial role, where our names also played a crucial role, and where the words in the distilled statement must be positive affirmations.

And, the trainer continued, "*Never* won't work here. Adverbs don't create images, so the subconscious pushes them out of the way and goes to the next word. In your case, that word is *late*. So, what we have here is a statement that says, My name is Judy Zerafa and I am late!"

With sweeping gestures and a big sarcastic smile, he continued. "The word *never* is a prompt that encourages you to write words that describe how you don't want to be. You end up creating a negative image. And that image sustains the negative habit. So, you have just reaffirmed your bad habit of being late."

> **What you want to create is an affirmation that will support exactly how you want to behave.**

Everyone laughed but me. "I don't think that's funny," I said.

"I'm sure you don't," the trainer said with a smile. "Let's see how we can make this work, okay? What you want to create is an affirmation that will support exactly how you want to behave. Explain to me in more precise terms *how* you want to be in relation to this time problem."

In that second, I got it! I looked at him with considerable confidence and said enthusiastically, "I, Judy Zerafa, am ALWAYS on time!"

"Bingo!" the trainer exclaimed. "She's got it!"

The final step, he said, was to hand-write our statements and then read what we had written, out loud to ourselves, twice a day. He stressed the importance of involving the senses of seeing and hearing when following the process.

I went home that evening and wrote my statement on a 3x5 card. Before falling asleep, I read my card out loud. As soon as the alarm rang the next morning, I picked up my card and read it out loud again. It didn't work. I was late getting my children to school and getting myself to work.

I remembered what the trainer had said about giving it time. Every night and every morning I continued to read that card aloud. With enthusiasm! After a week or so, there came a day when everything ... fell ... into ... place. "Wow!" I thought. "This is cool!"

The next day, we were late again. Eventually, however, I began to have weeks when I was on time (or even early!) as often as I was late. Then, I started seeing I was on time more than I was late. After six months ... well ... *I was a believer!* I have been doing what I came to call HABIT CARDS for about 25 years now. I can say with absolute honesty that, after that first year, I have been late only 3 times in the past 24 years. My reputation for being on time is stellar!

Over the years, I've used this strategy to change many habits. I've also used it to simply create behaviors I believed would make my life easier and better. Whenever I teach this Key, I tell people the HABIT CARD strategy is the closest thing to magic they will ever see.

> **The final step, he said, was to hand-write our statements and then read what we had written, out loud to ourselves, twice a day.**

I've been teaching audiences how to improve their lives with HABIT CARDS for more than two decades, and I've never had an audience that wasn't skeptical. The whole idea sounds so silly. I imagine as you read this you will feel the same skepticism. That's okay. Try it anyway! Think of one habit you want to get rid of. Get a clear understanding of how you want to behave and be perceived by your self and others within that particular issue.

If it helps to write your thoughts, do so. If you are able to think it through, that's okay, too.

Once you have a clear picture of how, or who, you want to be, write an enthusiastic, first-person, present-tense statement of exactly what you want.

Once again, a HABIT CARD always starts with the word *I*. Your *first and last names* follow. **The fourth word must be one of these three: am – only – always. A combination works too: am only – am always**. This fourth word, or combination of words, is the key to making sure what follows is what you want. While the adverbs *only* and *always* do not create an image themselves, they prompt the words that follow, guaranteeing the creation of a positive image. Here are examples of HABIT CARDS correctly written and highly likely to deliver the desired result:

I, (your first and last names), am always on time for everything!
I always arrive with time to spare!

I, (your first and last names), always have a positive attitude!
I check my attitude regularly and change it when necessary!

I, (your first and last names), am always kind, respectful and considerate!
I treat people as I want them to treat me!

I, (your first and last names), only crave healthy food and drinks.
I always quit eating as soon as I feel full!

Avoid using the following words: not, never, should, could, need to, will, going to, have to, or any contraction ending with n't. These words don't work, either because they throw the statement into the wrong tense (remember, your sentence *must be* in the present tense), or because they are easily followed by other words that will create a negative image. When you use the words *always* and *only*, you set up your statement to deliver a positive image.

KEY 3

There is no limit to the number of HABIT CARDS your subconscious mind can work on at any given time. The only consideration is the amount of time you have to read them each morning and night.

Once I experienced my own success with this strategy, I wanted to understand precisely how this process worked. Here's what I learned: In the beginning, when I started reading my HABIT CARD aloud, my subconscious mind became confused because I was making a statement about my self that was in dramatic contrast to the multi-layered image it had of me with regard to time. It dismissed what I was saying because there were more layers to the subconscious image than there were times when it had heard my contrasting statement.

After a few times of hearing me read, *"I, Judy Zerafa, am always on time"* with such enthusiasm, my subconscious was compelled to remove one of the overlays each time it heard me read that card. The contrast between what I was saying, and the number of layers on the image, became less and less. I kept my practice of reading that card twice a day. Each reading removed another layer of the self-defeating image.

Eventually, the enormous stack of overlays to that original image – the one I had formed as a child of someone who was always late – dwindled to the point where this habit was no longer one of the most developed images in that part of my mind. My subconscious paid less and less attention to making sure I matched my behavior to the image of me always being late.

Still, I kept reading that HABIT CARD every day! I wanted to erase every last overlay as well as the original image ... and replace it with a new image of my self as someone always on time. I wanted to add as many overlays as possible to that new image. I wanted my subconscious to work as hard at keeping me on time as it had worked to make me late.

In his 1990 book *What to Say When You Talk to Yourself*, Shad Helmstedder, Ph.D., explains that our subconscious minds are most suggestible to change as we are falling asleep at night and again as we are awakening in the morning. HABIT CARDS are, therefore, most effective if read at those two times. According to Dr. Helmstedder, there is no way of knowing when the original image has been removed.

For that reason, I urge my audiences to keep repeating their HABIT CARDS until they feel certain that the new, positive habit has taken the place of the self-defeating one, and there are sufficient overlays to guarantee their subconscious attention is highly focused on the new, self-empowering habit.

The subconscious mind works around the clock, gathering information from our environment and circumstances in an effort to support our most developed habits – both positive and negative. As explained previously, the subconscious mind is nearly one million times more powerful than the conscious mind. It is capable of extraordinary effort and manipulation of both our conscious mind and our bodies in order to keep our behavior consistent with our most developed images.

Back to the example of an overweight image: If your image of your self is that of being overweight and you've tried to diet, what do you experience as you consciously work to control what you eat? Do you often feel strong cravings or hunger pangs? Can you see now *why* you are having these and *what* is causing you to experience this? Your subconscious is just doing its job! It is doing whatever it takes to force you into behavior that is in sync with the image of your being overweight. The more developed your overweight image is, the harder your subconscious mind works to make sure you don't get out of sync.

If you are someone who has a subconscious image (habit) of being organized and something happens to cause clutter or chaos in your life, how do you feel? Anxious? Guess where that feeling of anxiety comes from! Your subconscious mind creates it to push you back into behavior (organizing everything) that in turn puts you back in focus with your image of being organized.

> **The subconscious mind is nearly one million times more powerful than the conscious mind.**

The habits we develop and build through the positive thoughts and feelings we have about our selves, as well as the positive perceptions we accept as truth from others, drive our subconscious minds to prompt and maintain corresponding behaviors *with little conscious effort on our part.* In other words: Positive habits shift the workload from our conscious effort to our subconscious servant. A powerful way to remember this concept is to think of the subconscious as our *servant* when a positive habit is involved, and as our *master* when a negative habit is involved.

To help your child or children create powerful, positive images (habits), encourage them to talk about themselves in powerful, positive words. Encourage them to say things like:
- I am a great test-taker!
- I always do my best!
- I am always kind and fair!
- I am organized!
- I am healthy and strong!

Find every opportunity to point out the good in your son or daughter. In fact, you have an incredible opportunity to foster powerful, supportive images in every relationship you have by finding the good in others and taking the time to sincerely express your positive perceptions of them.

FACTS TO REMEMBER

- Habits run your life.
- Every positive habit you put in place makes your life easier ... and better.
- Using Key 1 (A Positive Attitude) will help you say, feel and believe positive things about your self.
- Discovering your talents and abilities (Key 2) gives you specific subjects and activities you can then support by creating positive subconscious images (habits).

Family Activities

We hope you have fun teaching your children the GO FOR IT! Seven Keys to Success along *Your Path To An EASIER & BETTER Life*. Remember, children learn most readily by example. As a parent, your example is the most powerful and you can be sure your child is watching and learning. The more you work to incorporate the Seven Keys into your own life, the greater the chances are that your children will embrace and adopt them into their lives.

Below are some suggestions for family activities that will help demonstrate the process for replacing self-defeating habits with self-enhancing ones.

The goal of this chapter is for each family member to understand how habits are developed, how to erase those that are self-defeating and replace them with those that are positive and empowering. At this point, you should be able to see how the Keys are connecting to each other. Encourage family members to talk about what each has learned. Look for opportunities to connect Key 3 back to Keys 1 and 2.

In preparation for this session, make sure each family member has at least three 3x5 cards.

Start the Family Activities by having each person open his and her notebook to the first clean page. At the top of the page, write "Key 3 – Activities."

> **In other words:
> Positive habits shift the workload from our conscious effort to our subconscious servant.**

1. Have each person write two habits he or she feels are positive, habits that help toward being the person each wants to be. When everyone is finished writing, take turns reading these positive habits aloud.

2. Ask everyone to write one negative habit that he or she would like to erase. Explain that everyone will be asked to read this notebook entry aloud. Take turns doing so. Encourage everyone to respond respectfully and helpfully as each family member shares what he or she has written.

3. Have everyone write a description of how he or she wants to act, be, and be perceived by others with regard to the negative habit each wants to erase. Once again, everyone will have a chance to read this notebook entry aloud.

4. In your own words, explain the process for creating a HABIT CARD, or read the explanation that begins at the top of page 59. Ask each person to create a HABIT CARD that represents what he or she has written in the previous exercise. Ask each person to read the HABIT CARD he or she has written. As the leader, you will be listening to make sure each HABIT CARD has been written correctly.

5. Explain how important it is that everyone read the HABIT CARD right after awakening in the morning and just before going to sleep at night. If possible, create a chart with everyone's name across the top of a page. Down the left side of the page start with the date on which you start using your HABIT CARDS and end with the date 30 days hence. Have each person draw an X in the morning if he or she has read the card that morning and the night before. After 30 days, ask everyone to share his and her progress. Encourage everyone to continue reading the cards until everyone feels certain of having created a powerful, multi-layered image of how he or she wants to be. (Your example of sticking with this exercise will be very encouraging and supportive to your family members' continued effort.)

> **Explain how important it is that everyone read the HABIT CARD right after awakening in the morning and just before going to sleep at night.**

6. Have everyone in the family watch for other family members behaving in harmony with what they've written on their HABIT CARD. Reinforce family members by saying what you observed. For example, your child has written a card that says, *I, (first and last names),* *always go to bed on time!* When you see that happening, say something along the lines of, "I'm so proud of how you get to bed on time! Way to go!" or, "You seem rested and ready to do your best today! Good job with your positive habit of always going to bed on time!"

7. Discuss a habit you are interested in creating as a family. Ask each person to contribute to the decision of what that habit might be. Once you have come to a conclusion, create a HABIT CARD that enthusiastically words the habit. Each person will write his or her names, followed by a phrase that indicates the family. Example: *I, (first and last names), as a member of the Brown family, always do my best to keep our home safe and clean.* Encourage everyone to read his and her personal HABIT CARD and the family HABIT CARD for the next 30 days.

8. Before this session ends, have each person share something positive that has happened to him or her as a result of using Keys 1 or 2 in the past week.

WISE CHOICES

Choices Create Personal Power

How to Make choices that Bring Desired Results

KEY 4

Fundamentals

- Personal power comes from making wise choices every day.
- Proactive choices are made when we consciously decide ahead of time the result we want to experience. When a proactive choice is made with our best interest in mind, the choice *will move us forward*.
- Reactive choices are frequently initiated by subconscious images (habits). A reactive choice prompted by a positive habit *moves us forward;* a reactive choice prompted by a self-defeating habit *holds us back*.
- Every choice we make, whether proactive or reactive, produces a result that matches the choice.
- Failure to understand the relationship between choices and results is what causes us to feel like a victim.
- Making wise choices leads to greater freedom and opportunity in all areas of our lives.

What is a wise choice?

A wise choice is any choice that moves us in the direction we want to go, creating the result we desire. When making wise choices, and then experiencing their positive results, we become aware of our personal power.

Just as we are generating attitude every moment we are awake, we are also making choices every moment. Social research tells us that 98% of the time, we make our choices *reactively*. Only rarely do we think ahead to the outcome we desire and become *proactive* in consciously making choices we believe will bring the desired result. Reactive choices generated by positive habits move us forward and make our lives easier. Reactive choices generated by self-defeating habits, however, take away our personal power and make our lives more difficult and challenging. This is true for all of us at every age.

Feelings of victimhood are what we experience when we have not learned the relationship between a choice we've made and the unwanted consequences that follow.

As adults, we can make sure our children learn this important distinction early in their lives by pointing out the connection between the choices they are making and the experiences that make them feel fulfilled and happy … and those that do not. When you see your children experiencing the consequence of choices that have made them feel happy or proud, emphasize that it was their choices that made them feel this way. When they are dissatisfied with what they are experiencing, ask them to explain what they chose that made them feel this way. If they are unable to tell you, explain what you think the unwise choice was … without judgment. Simply provide the facts in words your child will understand. To make sure your son or daughter understands what you are saying, have your child repeat your words back to you.

A wise choice is any choice that moves us in the direction we want to go, creating the result we desire.

KEY 4

It is only when we understand the connection between what we choose and the experiences we are having that we can fully understand personal responsibility and power.

I've never seen a more dramatic example of understanding personal power than in an assembly of 200 fourth-grade students when I used their report cards as an example.

I asked the students who gave them the grades on their report cards. In unison they shouted, "My teacher!"

I asked how many of them could remember their grades from their last report card. Nearly all of them raised their hands. My next question was how many of them believed those grades were the very best they were capable of achieving. About 15% raised their hands. Then I asked how many knew in their hearts they were capable of receiving higher marks. The rest of the students raised their hands.

"How many of you who are proud of your last report card CHOSE to pay attention each day during class?" Not surprisingly, the students who were proud of their grades began to raise their hands after considering the question.

"How many of you who are proud of your last report card CHOSE to do your homework each day?" The same hands went up in the air.

"And ... how many of you ... when you knew there would be a test the next day ... CHOSE to prepare for that test?" The response was the same as above.

I paused for a moment and then dramatically explained, "See! You CHOSE to pay attention. You CHOSE to DO your homework. You CHOSE to prepare for your tests. The RESULT was a report card you were proud of!" All those students sat straighter in their chairs.

"How many of you who know you could have done better ... sometimes CHOSE not to pay attention in class?" Sheepishly and slowly, the hands of all the other students went up in the air.

He also mentioned how frequently the fourth-grade teachers talked about the way these students were becoming self-advocates.

I told them I was proud of them for their honesty, and that I had a couple of other questions. "How many of you who know you could have done better ... sometimes CHOSE not to do your homework?" Those same hands went up.

"And ... one last question: How many of you who know you could have done better ... sometimes CHOSE not to prepare for a test even when you knew it was coming?" All those same hands were in the air again.

"You made those choices and then your teachers recorded the results of your choices. Those results are the grades you received on your report cards."

The room became very quiet as the majority of the students who had made unwise choices slumped into their seats. *"How many of you would like to decide today what grades you want to see on your next report card?" I asked.*

The teachers, visiting parents, school administrators and I felt the excitement as we watched these fourth-graders collectively come to an understanding of their power to choose the grades on their report cards. Every hand in the room was raised. In that same moment, every adult watched 200 little spines straighten. The students sat taller. They were focused and quiet. You could see by their body language they were feeling empowered.

The students were told that when they returned to their classrooms, they would have the opportunity to choose the grades they wanted to receive on their next report card. They would be given a piece of paper with their name on it and a list of all the subjects they were taking. There would be two columns next to the list of subjects. The first column would show the grade they had received in each subject on their last report card. Next to those grades would be a blank space where they would write the grade they wanted to see for that subject on their next report card. They would be asked to *choose* each grade carefully after considering what they believed they were capable of achieving.

I reminded the fourth-grade students before they left the assembly that knowing what you want ahead of time makes it easy to make wise choices.

Six months later, as that school year was ending, I spoke with the principal. He said his fourth-graders had done an amazing job with our challenge of choosing their grades ahead of time. Their teachers had made copies of the grades they had chosen and taken time to write notes on their homework papers each week, letting them know if they were on track with their choices. The principal said these students had become the school leaders. He also mentioned how frequently the fourth-grade teachers talked about the way these students were becoming self-advocates.

Learning to make choices that are in our best interest (wise choices) is a critical step in building self-respect. It is also an

important step in developing leadership.

As a parent, you have opportunities every day to praise your children for making wise choices. When the choices they make are not in their best interest, you can help them understand how to make other choices that will be.

I had a father tell me he frequently used examples of his own choices, both wise and not so wise, to demonstrate the power of this Key. I believe that was a great strategy because it not only provided examples of how choice works, but also created an environment of honesty and openness between himself and his son.

It is okay to let our children see we aren't perfect; it is important to let them know we don't expect them to be perfect either. As a family, we just want everyone to try to do his and her very best each day. To underscore this point, here's a story I use to emphasize the importance of making wise choices.

THE BRICK STORY
by Judy Zerafa

Once upon a time, there were two young boys playing a game of jacks on the sidewalk in front of the houses in which they lived. It was a perfect summer day without a cloud in the sky! The boys were equally skilled at this game, so the competition was lively. All of a sudden, a stranger appeared. He was smiling and holding both hands behind his back. As he got close to the boys, he leaned down and extended his left hand to the first boy. The boys looked at each other, both puzzled. In his hand, the stranger seemed to be holding a brick. The first boy looked up at the stranger wondering what he was supposed to do. Without a word, the stranger leaned closer, indicating he wanted the boy to take the brick from his hand. The boy accepted the brick then examined it carefully. It was a brick. Just an ordinary brick.

The boy was not at all interested in what he had been given. With a bored look on his face and a shrug of his shoulder, he tossed the brick into his yard and indicated it was time to resume the game. The brick hit the ground and shattered into a dozen pieces.

The stranger looked sad, but then he turned toward the second boy, extending his other hand. In it was another brick. The second boy, equally anxious to get back to the game, accepted this odd gift. He examined it and determined it was just what it appeared to be: an ordinary brick, nothing special. The second boy, however, stood up and carried the brick to his own yard, where he carefully placed it on the ground. Without the boys noticing, the stranger disappeared as quickly and qui-

KEY

4

> As a family, we just want everyone to try to do his and her very best each day.

etly as he had arrived.

The two boys went back to their game. They played for the rest of that day until they were called in for dinner. Before saying goodbye, they agreed to spend the next day together.

The following morning, as the first boy got out of bed, he tripped and stubbed his toe on something. He looked down and saw it was a brick! Somehow, while he was asleep, another brick had been delivered. With his toe throbbing, the first boy bent, picked up the new brick, carried it to the window and tossed it onto the ground below, where it shattered like the one from the day before.

Next door, the second boy was just waking up, too. He got out of his bed and tripped over the brick that had mysteriously been delivered to him! The second boy bent, picked up the brick and carried it carefully to his yard, where he placed it alongside the one from the day before.

Every day for the next 70 years, both boys awakened each morning to discover a brand new brick.

In that seventieth year, the stranger reappeared and searched until he found the man who had once been that first little boy. He knocked on the door. When the old man answered, the stranger said, "I've come to see what you've done with all those bricks I've delivered over your lifetime."

The old man, bent over with age, had a very crabby look on his face when he replied, "Come. I will show you."

The old man shuffled uncomfortably to the window, drew back the covering, and in a voice that matched the crabby look on his face, he said, "There!"

The stranger looked where the old man was pointing. He gasped...and tears formed in his eyes as he looked at a moun-

> **KEY 4**
>
> **Decide today what you want to create with your life ... and you will know what choices to make with each new day.**

tain of rubble, made up entirely of broken and fragmented bricks. He shook his head in sadness and silently walked away.

The stranger searched until he found the other man who had once been the second little boy. He knocked at the door. When the old man answered, the stranger said, "I've come to see what you've done with all those bricks I've delivered over your lifetime."

This man was also bent over with age, but his voice was kind when he said, "Come. I will show you!"

Pulling himself up as tall and straight as he could, this old man walked toward his window, drew back the covering and pointed with pride. "There!" he said.

The stranger looked where the old man was pointing. He gasped. His eyes sparkled with joy. There before him was the most magnificent brick skyscraper he had ever seen! The stranger smiled, shook his head up and down, and said with great enthusiasm, "Well done! Well done!"

Those bricks are the days of our lives. Each morning we awaken to a brand new day. We get to choose what we do and how we do it every minute of each day! When we choose not to do our best with today, we have thrown this day away. Thrown-away days, like broken bricks, can't create anything but litter or trash. When we choose to try our best today; to give our very best effort in all we do, we are adding to the creation of a magnificent lifetime, one that will bring joy to our self, as well as respect and admiration from others. Decide today what you want to create with your life … and you will know what choices to make with each new day.

The Brick Story: Key Connections

No one but us gets to choose how we will live each day. We are the only ones who can make that choice. We need to teach our children they have the power to choose to have a good life; to make a difference; to earn the respect of others. Proactively deciding how we want to be and how we want to live makes it much easier to make choices that will deliver our desired results.

In a classroom where I was teaching Key 4 one day, a fifth-grade boy said he dreamed of growing up and playing in the NFL. I told him I thought that was an exciting dream, but wanted to know how serious he was. I asked him where NFL players come from. He looked puzzled for a second or two, and then one of his classmates said, "Pro scouts visit colleges and recruit the best players."

"That sounds right," I said. "So … how do you get into college?"

"You have to graduate from high school and then get accepted to a college with a good football team," one of the girls answered.

"How do you get into a college with a good football team?"

"My brother says you have to have good grades in high school so you are eligible to play sports. Then you have to keep your grades up and work hard to be a good football player," another girl responded. "Our dad told my brother he needs to get good grades all through school to make sure he has that chance."

"So … you are in fifth grade now … are there any choices you could be making today that would improve your chances of this happening?" I asked.

Everyone had an idea! They talked about making choices for getting good grades *now* to make it easier to do well in high school. They talked about making wise food choices to build a healthy body. They said it was important to choose to learn the rules of the game and watch the pros play. Someone said it would be a good choice to go to bed on time every night so as to get enough sleep. They talked about choosing to work out and stay fit, instead of sitting on the couch watching television.

Their teacher jumped into the conversation and asked questions about how much pro football players make. She explained how important it is for athletes to read well and be good at math so they will understand the contracts being offered, and know what percentage of their monies will go to paying their agent and other people who will be working for them. This was turning into an exciting conversation. *Now* these students were connecting those important dots between being a good student in the fifth grade and their opportunities for making their dreams come true in the future!

One of the class realists pointed out how slim the chances were of actually being picked to be an NFL player. This was a perfect place to connect this Key back to the others...particularly Key 2. I turned to the boy who said he dreamed of being an NFL player. I told him I hoped he made that dream come true, but that if he didn't, I was sure there were other careers he could aim for that would keep him close to football.

Everyone got into this discussion! We listed jobs related to football … a sports announcer, a sports agent, a referee, a coach, a trainer, sports doctor, football equipment manager, stadium worker, college scout. Magic happened in that classroom that day as these students came to understand how their choices could open the doors to who they wanted to be and how they wanted to live.

When the bell rang ending that class, everyone was fired up and seemed to have a new attitude. They decided to create a Habit Card as a class. They were going to start and end each hour by saying aloud, *I, (their names), always make wise choices!*

KEY 4

Proactively deciding how we want to be and how we want to live makes it much easier to make choices that will deliver our desired results.

What could be more exciting than watching your child take responsibility for making good things happen in his or her life? The earlier children learn how important all their choices are and how to make wise ones, the better their lives will be, and the less time you will spend worrying about them.

Take time as you eat together, ride in the car, or take a walk, to talk with your children about what they want to achieve or how they want to feel at the end of this day, this week, or this year. Have them tell you what choices they need to make to guarantee those results.

FACTS TO REMEMBER

Wise choices are easier to make with:
- a positive attitude – Key 1
- belief in one's self – Key 2
- positive habits – Key 3

Family Activities

We hope you have fun teaching your children the GO FOR IT! Seven Keys to Success along *Your Path To An EASIER & BETTER Life*. Remember, children learn most readily by example. As a parent, your example is the most powerful example in their lives. You can be sure your child is watching and learning. The more you work to incorporate the Seven Keys into your life, the greater the chances are that your children will embrace and adopt them into their lives.

Below are suggestions for family activities to help you make choices that create personal power – choices that bring desired results.

KEY 4

Review homework assignments and teacher comments regularly to ensure your child is making choices that will bring the desired result.

1. **Have all family members** open their notebooks to the first blank page and write "Key 4 – Activities" at the top of the page.

2. **Ask them to write** one thing in their lives that is making them feel proud or happy. Take turns, with each person sharing aloud what he or she has written.

3. **Have them write** at least two wise choices they have made that brought the positive results they have just shared with everyone.

4. **Then ask each person** to write one thing about his or her circumstances that is not leading to happy or proud feelings. Ask everyone

to take turns sharing his or her notebook entry aloud. Remind the family that it is important to show respect to one another.

5. Have each member list two choices each has made that produced unwanted results. Again, encourage all family members to treat each other as each wants to be treated.

6. Ask everyone to look at his or her answer to Exercise 4 and consider two choices that, had they been made, would have produced a better result. Ask everyone to write his or her answers in the notebook, and then take turns sharing.

7. Encourage everyone to think of someone he or she believes makes wise choices. Give everyone an opportunity to explain whom he or she picked and what that person's wise choices are.

8. Have school-age children tear out one sheet of paper from their notebooks. On that page, ask them to list the subjects they are studying in school and, next to each subject, the grade from their last report card. Next to that grade, have your child write the grade he or she wants to receive on the next report card. Be sure to encourage your child to be realistic. If, for example, the math grade was low (such as a D) last time, it might not be realistic to expect a top grade this time. Encourage your child to see that, with wise choices and work, it will probably be possible to earn an average grade, or even a better than average grade.

Once the grades have been chosen and put on paper, post these choices on the refrigerator or other prominent place as a reminder to check in with your son or daughter often. Review homework assignments and teacher comments regularly to ensure your child is making choices that will bring the desired result. If your child is in elementary school, and the two of you agree, you may want to schedule an appointment or phone call with the teacher to explain what you are doing with this exercise and ask for the teacher's support in helping your child succeed. If your child is in middle or high school, this might be a good opportunity to encourage him or her to make that appointment or phone call asking for support.

9. Between now and your next family session, encourage everyone to catch each other making wise choices and cheer one another on!

KEY 4

KEY
4

SETTING AND ACHIEVING GOALS

Live Your Dreams

How to Set And Achieve Goals

Fundamentals

- An unwritten goal is only a wish; a written goal is a commitment.
- Most goals are reached one step at a time.
- Successful people are those who understand the importance of setting goals and working toward them in all areas of their lives.

What is the difference between a goal and a wish?

According to the Merriam-Webster dictionary, a goal is "the end toward which effort is directed." A wish is described as "an object of desire." In other words, a goal is something we are willing to work toward, but a wish is something we would simply like to have happen.

What is the most effective way to set a goal?

In 1980, a research project was undertaken in which 200 graduating seniors from Harvard University were asked if they had goals. All these young men and women said they did have goals and agreed to be interviewed regularly over the next two decades to report their progress.

In 2000, the project ended, and the results were published two years later. The research showed that only 7 of the 200 participants had reached, or were significantly on track to reach, their individual goals. The most significant correlation shared by these 7 people was the fact that they had written their goals on paper; the other 193 people had not.

The Harvard project is one of many over the years in which a direct link exists between writing a goal on paper ... and achieving that goal. Science defines this process as *neuro-linguistic programming*. Research in the field of setting and reaching goals has provided significant evidence of the power of neuro-linguistic programming with regard to goal achievement.

Here's what happens when we write our goals on paper: The act of writing a goal on paper turns on a part of the brain known as the reticular activator. Our *reticular activator* is a cluster of cells in the brainstem that acts as a filter for information. Every day, we are bombarded by many tens of thousands of sensory perceptions. Our reticular activator sorts all the information delivered to our senses and alerts us to what we need to notice based on what is important to us. Our reticular activator keeps us from having to pay attention to information (or sensory stimuli) that is not important to us. If we didn't have reticular activators, we would be overwhelmed by too much information, and be unable to function mentally, physically or emotionally. Our reticular activator is the first line of defense in protecting us from information overload.

Whether your goal is something big that might take years to reach, or something little you want to accomplish today, writing your goal on paper gets your reticular activator involved, ready to provide extra help toward achieving your goal ... no matter how big or small it might be.

> **In other words, a goal is something we are willing to work toward, but a wish is something we would simply like to have happen.**

The way I found the perfect exercise machine is a good example of how the reticular activator works.

During my annual physical a couple of years ago, my doctor asked if I was working out regularly. I told him I was so busy I frequently skipped the long walks I had been in the habit of taking ... and besides, it was winter and there was so much ice!

"No excuses!" my doctor said as he shook his head. "If you're not going to walk every day, then get yourself into a gym or buy an exercise bike."

I'm not a gym person. I like to exercise alone. I was not going to buy an exercise bike because I didn't have the space it would require. But I definitely knew I needed to do something.

That night, I opened my Goal Journal. (Yes. I have a notebook just for my goals.) I thought about my options. No gym. No stationary bike. Something that doesn't take up much space and costs no more than X. I wrote my goal in my journal and I *knew* from years of experience that my reticular activator would help me with my goal.

That weekend, I had a long list of errands to run. I headed toward the mall. A couple of miles from my house, on the same street I'd driven for the past 10 years, I noticed a store sign I'd never seen before. It was for a home exercise equipment store. I crossed the intersection, put on my turn signal, and pulled into the parking lot.

It was a big place with lots of bikes, treadmills and weight training equipment. I walked up and down the aisles and didn't see anything that looked like it would fit in my small space. A salesman walked over and asked if he could help. I told him I wanted something that would give me a full-body cardio workout. It needed to be compact and within a certain price range. He pointed to a rowing machine that had a water cylinder attached. He offered to hold my coat and asked me to give it a try. I got situated on this strange-looking thing and did a few reps. I could definitely feel this was a machine that would deliver a full-body workout! I really liked how it worked. I did a few more reps, then got off. There was no way this weird-looking piece of equipment would fit in my house, however.

> **KEY 5**
>
> **Assertive Goals are those that give our lives a sense of purpose as we work toward their achievement, and they provide us with a feeling of fulfillment.**

"I think this is definitely the kind of thing I'm looking for," I explained, "but I'm afraid it won't fit in my place. I need something that doesn't take much space. Or something that can fold up and be stored in a closet."

The salesman laid my coat on a nearby counter, then reached down, placed the fingertips of his right hand under the cylinder and with no apparent effort stood the machine straight up. When the machine was upright, I noticed four small wheels under the bottom of the machine. He wrapped his fingers around the bar that held the seat and easily guided the now-upright machine toward a nearby wall. The Wave Rower now took less than a square foot of space!

"Wow! This is perfect!" I told him enthusiastically. Then I remembered my budget. The price tag was hanging from the top of the machine as it stood against the wall. I looked at it ... and couldn't believe my eyes. It was $10 less than the maximum amount I had set for myself. I picked up my coat and said, "You've got yourself a sale."

Are there different kinds of goals?

Merriam-Webster's on-line dictionary defines the word **passive** as **acted upon by an external agency; receptive to outside impressions or influences.** These phrases are very appropriate descriptors for a Passive Goal, which is something we desire, but don't choose to commit a lot of energy toward achieving. The key to reaching this kind of goal is knowing what we are looking to find, or accomplish, and then committing that knowledge to paper ... the crucial process of writing down any personal goal programs so that our reticular activator can locate information or opportunities necessary to accomplish the goal and make us aware of them. In the case of a Passive Goal, the reticular activator does the majority of the work. Our responsibility is to act on the information or opportunity it brings.

If you agree the word passive describes the kind of goal that is more a desire than a determination, then you will agree that the word *assertive* is the appropriate word for describing the latter. Merriam-Webster defines **assertive** as **having or showing bold forcefulness in the pursuit of a goal.** An Assertive Goal is one to which we commit sincere effort. Assertive Goals are those that give our lives a sense of purpose as we work toward their achievement, and they provide us with a feeling of fulfillment when we do achieve them.

Many of us believe we have to know ahead of time all the steps needed for accomplishing a particular goal. In fact ... the only thing we need to know in order to *set* a goal is *what we want*. We don't need to know all the hows, whens or whats before we start. All we need to start is being clear about what we want, and writing it on paper.

Once we've written down our goal, we have engaged our reticular activator, which then alerts us to the hows, whens and whats at the appropriate time.

Consciously committing to daily activity directed toward achieving our goal is what allows us to reap the greatest benefit from the effort of our reticular activator. It is when we are *in action* that we are most aware of this help.

The getting-to-the-chair example

At the GO FOR IT! Institute, we've discovered that the analogy of travel is an easy way to explain the setting and reaching of goals to children. In a recent fifth-grade class, we introduced this Key (*Setting and Achieving Goals*) by placing a chair at the back of the room. We explained that getting to that chair was the goal. We asked for six student volunteers to help demonstrate what it takes to reach a goal. We divided the students into two teams of three. The first team was called Wishers; the second team, Doers.

We explained to the Wishers that we wanted them to use all their mental and emotional power to get themselves to the back of the room and touch that chair. They were not allowed to use any physical power. At the count of three, they would be asked to close their eyes and wish with all their might! We encouraged the Wishers' classmates to cheer them on. It got noisy in that classroom! I counted slowly to 10 as we watched the Wishers huff and puff and wish and wish some more...At the count of 10, the Wishers opened their eyes. I asked if they had wished as hard as they possibly could. Everyone said Yes! I told them I believed them; I knew they had wished with all their might.

Now it was time for the Doers. I told this team their job was to get to the back of the room and touch the chair. I explained they could get to that chair any way they thought would work, but they couldn't copy what the person before them had done.

The first Doer skipped straight down the middle aisle of the classroom, touched the chair and bowed to enthusiastic applause. The second Doer jumped from the front of the room, down the left side of the room, halfway across the back of the room, then touched the chair and bowed. Her classmates whistled and clapped their approval. The third Doer stood sideways and did a sliding step in a zigzag pattern from the front of the room to the back. He touched the chair and bowed, once again to enthusiastic applause.

When everyone had quieted down, I asked the students who had done the exercise right. Most of the students said it was the first Doer; a few said it was the second. No one thought the third Doer had done it right.

I asked the students to explain their conclusions.

"The first Doer walked straight down the middle, directly to the chair," someone explained.

"I think the second Doer did it better because she jumped fast!" another classmate chimed in.

"So, why doesn't anyone think the third Doer was doing it right?" I asked.

"He took too long!" was the response.

"What was the goal?" I asked everyone.

"To get to the back of the room and touch the chair!" everyone shouted.

"So-o-o-o … didn't the third Doer accomplish that?" I asked.

Slowly, everyone agreed.

"We're all different," I explained. "We do things differently. Some of us are faster than others. We have different learning styles.

"The goal of this demonstration was to get to the back of the room and touch the chair. Each of the Doers did that in his or her own way…but each of them *did* reach the goal. They each approached the goal from different directions; each of them took a different amount of time. The only thing they had in common was that they *did* something. Each of the Doers took action toward reaching his or her goal."

> **Once we've written down our goal, we have engaged our reticular activator, which then alerts us to the hows, whens and whats at the appropriate time.**

KEY 5

How many steps to Orlando?

That classroom was in Denver, Colorado, where the GO FOR IT! Institute has its office. To reinforce the lesson about setting and reaching goals, I asked the students if they thought it was possible to get from where we were in Denver to Disney World in Orlando, Florida. Everyone agreed it was.

"How can we get from Denver to Orlando?" I asked. The answers included taking a plane, going by bus, train or car. One girl said you could ride a bike. It would take a long time to pedal from Denver to Orlando, but it could be done! Someone suggested you could even walk from Denver to Orlando. "That's true." I agreed. "It is possible to get from Denver, Colorado to Orlando, Florida on foot.

"So," I continued, "our goal is to get to Orlando." Once we set this goal, it became clear we would need to decide *how* we would travel. We considered our options, and chose to travel by plane.

"What do you think we need to do next?" I asked.

"I think we need to figure out how much money we will need," someone said.

"How do we do that?" I asked.

"You could look on the Internet. Or you could call the airlines and the hotels," a student suggested.

> KEY
> 5
> **"Setting and reaching goals is somewhat like learning to ride a bike. You get better at it the more you try."**

"Great idea. Does that sound like the logical next step?" I asked.

"Yeah. Unless we already had a lot of money, we'd need to figure out how much this is going to cost."

"This is exactly how goal-setting works," I explained. "You figure out *what you want* first. Then you think about what you could do next. That is the second step ... in this case it is figuring out how much the plane fare and rooms will cost. Afterwards, what do you think might be the next step?" I asked.

"We would each have to decide how we are going to earn the money we need," one of the quieter students chimed in.

"And after that?" I asked. "What would the next step be?"

"Pick a date and then make reservations!" someone shouted.

"Perfect!" I responded. "I can tell that all of you understand that getting to our goal of visiting Orlando will take a lot of steps. If I had asked you to take a blank sheet of paper and list everything you would need to do, in the exact order it would need to be done, in order to get to Orlando, how many of you think you could have figured it out on the spot?"

Not one hand went up.

"That's okay!" I assured them. "How many of you could have thought of one step in the process?"

Everyone raised a hand.

"That's how the process works! **You start by deciding what you want. Then, write that goal on paper. Once you've taken these first two steps, you will figure out what step to take next.**"

"What if you can't figure it out," asked one of the girls.

"Let's think about that. Anybody got any ideas?" I asked.

There was a brief pause, and then some said they would ask other people if they had ever traveled to Florida and find out what they had to do to get there.

"That's a great idea. In fact, I think that would be a logical next step. No matter what goal you are trying to achieve, you may get stuck along the way. You may not be able to figure out what you should do next. That's a perfect time to ask for help!"

I paused, then asked, "How many of you know how to ride a bike?"

Everybody's hand went up.

"Are you pretty good at bike riding?"

"Sure!" was the general answer.

"Did you always ride well?"

Lots of laughter here as some of the students explained how many times they fell off before they were able to ride with confidence.

"Setting and reaching goals is somewhat like learning to ride a bike. You get better at it the more you try. You develop instincts that help you to avoid falling over. Now, sometimes when you're out riding, do you ever find yourself taking a detour when something gets in the way?"

Everyone nodded, or said yes!

"It's exactly the same with goals. There will be times when you set

KEY
5

a goal and you're going in the right direction, making a lot of progress. All of a sudden, something happens and you're stuck ... or realize something is in your way. You stop and consider what you can do to get around the obstacle in your path.

"You will probably never meet anyone who hasn't had to stop and reconsider at least one step on the journey toward a goal. Most people do occasionally experience the need for a detour or a re-focus when they are working on their goals. The important thing isn't how long it takes to reach a goal; how many detours along the way; or how many stops and starts. The important thing is that you *have* a goal; that you are taking action, working, moving *toward* achieving some thing or event."

Then I asked the class, "Why did you want to learn to ride a bike when you were younger?"

"So I could get places!" one of the boys answered.

"How many of you enjoy being able to go places?" I asked.

No one answered immediately. They looked around the room at one another, smiling tentatively and shrugging their shoulders. A boy in the back of the room finally said, "Yeah. I like going places. I don't want to be in the same place all the time."

"Setting goals takes you places. Each time you set a goal, and then reach it, you have a new experience. You find out more about yourself and learn what you are capable of achieving. Goals are what give meaning to your life. Maybe this story will explain it better," I said.

THE HOCKEY GOALS
by Judy Zerafa

There's a little town in Michigan where hockey is all anyone talks about during the school season. There are two high schools in this town, each with a competitive hockey team. The coaches are brothers. Paul went to one high school; Jake went to the other. Both were star players for their respective teams. When they graduated, Paul went to a college out East and played hockey during his undergraduate years. Jake went to school in the Midwest and did the same. After college graduation, both brothers returned to Michigan and began their careers as high school teachers ... and hockey coaches at their respective alma maters. The two brothers talked often about how much they had learned from playing sports. While they had always been fierce competitors, they were also the best of friends.

Paul and Jake taught core classes, which gave them an opportunity to really know the kids on their particular hockey teams. With this much contact every week, these coaches were able to understand their players' capabilities ... and some of their dreams. These two men were an inspiration to everyone who knew them.

> **"You will probably never meet anyone who hasn't had to stop and reconsider at least one step on the journey toward a goal.**
>
> **KEY 5**

There was no question that both schools had very talented hockey teams, but Paul and Jake knew that to be successful as adults, all these students would need more than athletic ability. Both brothers were always looking for ways to teach life-lessons whenever there was an opportunity.

One year, both hockey teams made it to division playoffs. The school rivalry was spirited and contagious. Of course each team wanted to beat the other and win the title, but everyone knew if either team was defeated before the championship game, the team that got eliminated would place its full support behind the one remaining in competition. Respect and sportsmanship were defined by every player on both teams ... thanks to the outstanding example and encouragement of the two brothers. There was a spectacular rivalry on the ice, but also a powerful sense of community spirit and pride.

As the playoffs neared, Paul and Jake took every opportunity to boost both the rivalry and community spirit by scheduling practices with each other's teams. As in a lot of small-town communities, parents and friends frequently showed up to cheer the teams on these occasions.

One evening near the end of the playoffs, Paul and Jake scheduled a practice between their teams that turned into an experience the players talked about for months and remembered for years. The evening started out as usual, with all players from both teams skating around the rink, warming up. Eventually, it was time for practice to start and the puck to drop. On a silent signal, both Paul and Jake skated from their respective benches onto the ice, each moving toward his team's goal cage. They moved in perfect unison to opposite ends of the ice. As they approached the cages, they stuck their hands out in front of them and began pushing the cages off the ice.

> KEY 5
>
> **"Exactly! What is the point in all of this activity if you don't know what you are aiming for!"**

The players, poised for the puck to drop, had no idea what was happening. They watched their coaches in confusion. Silently, they began looking at each other, passing a question from eye to eye. "What are they doing?" each player seemed to be asking. The fans were just as confused.

Once the goal cages were off the ice and out of sight, the two brothers skated to center ice as if nothing was wrong. They signaled for the puck to drop. All the players started shouting,

"Where are the goal cages?"

Very calmly, one of the brothers shrugged his shoulders and said, "We don't need the goal cages. Come on, let's get things started."

The boys didn't move. They had no idea what to do. One of the team captains said, "Coach, stop fooling around. How can we play without goal cages! How do we know if we've scored? How're we going to know who's won if there's no way to see who scores the most points?"

The coaches looked at all of their players. Then, as if on cue, they responded together. "Exactly! What is the point in all of this activity if you don't know what you are aiming for!"

Then, still speaking together, they added: "Boys, we want you to remember what you've experienced here tonight for the rest of your lives. It doesn't matter how hard you work if there is no goal. Everything worth having or doing in your life needs to be defined as a goal."

The goal cages were brought back onto the ice and the practice started. According to one of the players years later, no one remembered who *won* that night ... but everyone remembered what they *learned* that night.

KEY
5

The Hockey Goals: Key Connections

I asked the class what they learned from the story. Someone answered, "Setting goals is important!" Everyone agreed, and we returned to the exercise.

We had decided earlier in that hour that our goal would be to go to Orlando by plane. Our next step was to make a list of everything that would need to be taken care of before we would be ready to go to the airport and get on the plane.

The class came up with a list of important steps. To take a plane from Denver to Orlando, you would need to have enough money to pay for the flights and all the other expenses like food and a hotel room and the tickets to get into Disney World while you were there. You would need to decide on the clothes you would want to wear while you were gone; then you'd have to make sure those clothes were clean and packed in a suitcase. You would need to make reservations for your flights and book a hotel room. These fifth-graders were completely engaged in this exercise.

I asked the class how they thought the pilot would know how to get from Denver to Orlando. "Do you think the pilot would be able to just look out the window and see Orlando once he or she got the plane in the air?" I asked.

Everyone laughed.

"Well, if the pilot can't see where he's headed, how could you be sure you would get to Orlando?" I asked.

One of the girls explained that her uncle was a pilot. He had told her that the pilot gets instructions from the control tower explaining how high in the air he is supposed to fly. That is called "altitude." Once the pilot reaches altitude, he or she is given a "heading," which is like an invisible highway in the sky. Pilots know if they stay on these headings, they will reach their destination. The girl explained that, most of the time, the pilot can't see his or her final destination until it's close enough to start the descent to the airport runway.

"What your classmate just described is similar to what happens with most people and most of their goals. They begin by deciding what they want to accomplish. The next step is figuring out what has to be done first. With that first step, they are on the path moving toward their goal. They can't see the final destination, but they know the general direction. They gather information along the way and adjust for unexpected circumstances. They know they have to keep moving one step at a time. Eventually, you are close enough to see the goal. When you are close enough to see your goal, you understand that there is nothing complicated about reaching any goal. You do it *one step at a time.*"

We spent the rest of this class talking about things the students hadn't thought of as goals before, but things they knew they wanted to accomplish.

The students took turns telling the rest of us what they wanted to achieve. Someone wanted to be in the school's talent competition at the end of that year. Another wanted to save enough money to buy a bicycle. Some students couldn't identify anything specific. One boy, hiding out in the back row, looked unsure. I asked, "Is there something you'd like to do but aren't sure you could?"

I watched him take a deep breath and look at one of his classmates. He turned back toward me and said, "I want to go to college. No one in my family has ever gone. I want to be the first."

"Are any other students interested in going on to college?" I asked. About half the students raised their hands. "That's a big goal," I told them. "A big, important goal. There are a lot of steps to take in order to get into college. There are even more once you get in and set a goal to graduate. What would be one step you could take today that would move you in the right direction?"

> **They gather information along the way and adjust for unexpected circumstances. They know they have to keep moving one step at a time.**

KEY 5

"I think that is a goal you should write on paper," the boy in the back row answered. Everyone agreed. As the class ended, the students who wanted to go to college were taking turns going to the front of the room and writing on a whiteboard the steps they could be taking now to move themselves in the direction of being accepted by a college once they graduated from high school.

It is never too early to teach a child how to set goals and get on the path to achieving them. As Albert Einstein said, "If you want to live a happy life, tie it to a goal, not to people or things."

Because you are working on the Seven Keys to Success on *Your Path To An EASIER & BETTER Life,* you've already learned four strategies that make setting and achieving goals something everyone in your family can do: Having a positive attitude, discovering your talents and abilities, developing supportive habits and making wise choices ... all four strategies prepare you for achieving success with Key 5.

Outgrowing goals, sharing frustration

A final thought before we move on to Key 6: Children outgrow dreams and goals just as they outgrow shoes. One day, a pair of shoes fits just fine; the next day, those same shoes pinch and it's time for a new pair. (Adults sometimes outgrow shoes, too.) When our shoes no longer fit, we can feel it. Although we can't experience the pinch of outgrown shoes on our children, we are able to see the signs. Sometimes children tell us their feet hurt; sometimes we can tell by watching them walk. We get a sense of their discomfort. Like shoes, goals and dreams can be outgrown. Talking with your children about their goals and dreams gives you the opportunity to see if they have grown beyond what they used to want for themselves. If you see that they have, it's time to help them set their focus on something worthy of who they are *today* and invest their time and energy in something that's a better fit.

> **It is never too early to teach a child how to set goals and get on the path to achieving them.**

There is, of course, a big difference between outgrowing a goal ... and just wanting to give up out of frustration when the challenges, time or effort required become more than was anticipated. The desire to throw in the towel and call it quits before we reach our goal happens to most of us at some point along the way to the finish line.

When we're struggling with a goal as adults, it usually helps to talk through our frustration with someone we trust and respect. Getting our frustration outside ourselves by sharing it with another person gives us the perspective we need to decide if it's in our best interest to keep trying or whether it's time to move on and find a new goal.

Helping a child decide if he or she has outgrown a goal and needs to move on – or needs to re-focus, try harder and hang in there – is a decision more easily made if you have been talking with your child regularly about his or her goal. Listen with your eyes and heart as well as your ears. Watch body language. Get feedback from coaches, teachers or others involved in your son's or daughter's goal. In the end, however, your instincts as a parent will undoubtedly serve you best in reaching the right decision – especially if you both stay focused on Keys 1 through 4.

FACTS TO REMEMBER

Reinforce your effort – and your child's effort – in goal setting and achieving:

- **Key 1.** Whether you are working on setting a goal, working toward achieving a goal, or trying to decide if it is time to move on from a goal that has been outgrown or has lost its meaning, a *positive attitude* is what will help you most.

- **Key 2.** When you set a goal based on one of *your talents and abilities*, you are investing your time and effort in something in which you already have an interest. Personal interest generates enjoyment, and that keeps you motivated. Any effort you invest in a personal talent or ability adds value to that talent or ability.

- **Key 3.** You've learned *how to get rid of habits that hold you back, and how to develop habits that move you forward.* Using Key 3 makes it easier for you to reach your goal because it programs your subconscious to do a good share of the work required for reaching your goal.

- **Key 4.** When you set a personal goal, you have decided what you want. *Making wise choices* helps you see the next step you need to take along the way to achieving your goal.

KEY 5

Family Activities

We hope you have fun teaching your children the Seven Keys to Success along *Your Path To An EASIER & BETTER Life*. Remember, children learn most readily by example. As a parent, your example is the most powerful example in their lives. You can be sure your child is watching and learning. The more you work to incorporate the Seven Keys into your life, the greater the chances are that your children will embrace and adopt them into their lives.

Below are suggestions for family activities that will help you set goals individually and as a family.

1. Have all family members open their notebooks to the first blank page and write "Key 5 – Activities" at the top of the page.

2. Explain how the Reticular Activator helps in making us aware of information and opportunities that will move us in the direction of our goals. Review the explanation on *Passive Goals* and encourage everyone to write even his or her smallest goals on paper.

3. Go around the table (or wherever you are gathered) and make sure each person clearly understands the difference between a *wish* and a *goal*.

4. As the family member leading this session, if you have any doubt that your child or children may not clearly understand the difference between a wish and a goal, use the chair exercise explained in this chapter.

5. Have a discussion about wishing something would happen as opposed to taking action to make something happen. *Make sure everyone understands that reaching a goal does require action.*

6. Using their notebooks and the Key 5 – Activities page, have all family members list one individual goal they would like to accomplish. This can be a big-dream type of goal or something smaller that can be accomplished more quickly.

7. Take turns going around the table and have everyone share his or her goal.

8. Go back to the notebooks and have family members individually write as many steps as they can think of that will need to be taken once each starts working on his or her goal.

9. Have each family member share the steps he or she has written and encourage everyone else to comment. This kind of sharing usually helps everyone develop a better focus on the steps necessary to completing a goal.

10. Have everyone flip his or her notebook to the back. Thumb back five pages. At the top of this page, have each person write *My Goal Journal*. Then, on the first line have each person write the day's date; on that same line, have each person write the goal he or she has chosen. On the next line, have each person write the first step he or she will need to take in order to start moving toward the goal.

11. Explain that for the next 30 days, everyone is going to be responsible for taking one step toward his or her goal every day. At the end of each day, everyone should take a minute to write the day's date and briefly describe what that person has done that day to move closer to his or her goal.

> **Explain that for the next 30 days, everyone is going to be responsible for taking one step toward his or her goal every day.**

For example, if someone in your family has chosen the goal of becoming an accomplished piano player, the first step for that person might be to find someone who can teach them how to play the piano. Once he or she is enrolled in taking lessons, the amount of practice time each day should be recorded over this 30-day period. At the end of 30 days, get together for a family meal and give everyone the opportunity to talk about his or her progress.

Sharing progress toward their goal will give everyone a chance to acknowledge and celebrate the progress of each other.

12. Once everyone has had a chance to see that he or she is capable of setting and working toward a goal, consider working together as a family on a specific family goal. Take turns sharing ideas on what family members would like to accomplish as a team. Have someone act as the group's secretary and write all the suggestions on a piece of paper. Once everyone has had a chance to contribute, begin to narrow the list until you find a family goal you are each willing and capable of working to achieve.

Depending on the ages of the children, the following list might help you get started:

- Fixing one family meal together within the current month.
- Going on one fun family outing within the next month.
- Learning a new game together.
- Starting a family photo (or multimedia!) album.
- Planning for a family camping trip or a vacation within the next year.
- Making a family video to send to relatives living far away.
- Adopting a family pet.

The benefits of setting and achieving a family goal are exciting and important. There is nothing that will make your family closer or stronger than working together toward something you all want. The setting and the achieving of family goals build skills that will benefit everyone for the rest of his or her life.

Once the family goal has been set, your job as the family session leader on this Key is to make sure everyone has the opportunity to participate in a way that allows everyone to see his or her individual importance in reaching the family goal.

You don't have to have a big family for this to work! Even if there are only two of you, you ARE a team.

USING CREATIVE IMAGINATION

How to Use the Gift of Imagination to Accelerate Progress

Toward Goal Achievement and Personal Growth

Fundamentals

- Imagination is a unique gift to the human species.
- Imagination works like a muscle. The more it is used, the more powerful it becomes; the less it is used, the weaker it becomes.
- Imagination among young children is natural and highly developed.
- When children become socialized, they use their imagination less as they work to fit in with their peers and adapt to their culture.
- *Experiential Visualization* is a specific technique developed through imagination that accelerates progress toward achieving a goal.
- *Acting As If* is a technique developed through imagination to accelerate personal growth.
- There is scientific proof that imagination has the power to extend the physical body's achievement boundaries.
- The human body cannot distinguish an imagined experience from an actual experience.

What is imagination?

Merriam-Webster defines imagination as "the creative ability of forming a mental image of something not present to the senses or never before wholly perceived in reality."

The American inventor Charles Kettering described imagination as "the only limit to what we can hope to have in the future."

Everything that is man-made begins with imagination. The home in which you live; the car, train, bike, bus, plane in which you travel; the games you play; the books you read; the technology you enjoy ... all of these were built or developed through imagination.

Imagination is where all human advancement begins. When civilization moves forward, imagination is the fuel that propels it. The power of imagination is what sets mankind apart from all other forms of life. Imagination is one of the greatest human gifts.

We are born with imagination but, sadly, most of us don't fully understand the power of this gift or how to develop and use it. One way to help children understand imagination is by comparing it to our legs. The more we use our legs, the stronger they become. The stronger they become, the faster and farther they can carry us. Anyone who has ever had a broken leg and had to wear a cast understands how quickly legs can weaken. But once the cast is off and the leg is exercised regularly, it gets back into shape quickly.

Just like our legs, our imagination has the ability to take us where we want to go ... but it has to be exercised regularly to do its job. The more we use our imagination, the stronger it becomes.

How can we develop and use imagination?

There are two specific techniques for developing and strengthening imagination. The first is *Experiential Visualization*. This is a special way of using imagination to accelerate progress toward the achievement of a goal. For decades, this technique has been a significant part of sports training for serious athletes. Science has proven that the use of experiential visualization can significantly extend the physical ability of the human body. We now know this technique is valuable in the achievement of interpersonal, academic and economic goals.

The second technique for developing and using imagination is termed *Act As If*. This particular technique is highly effective in personal development.

As with all the other Keys to Success, this Key can be effectively used by very young children. In fact, Key 6 is just plain fun for people of any age!

How does experiential visualization work?

When I teach experiential visualization, I always ask those in the audience to close their eyes and play along with an exercise. It doesn't matter whether the participants are elementary students, seasoned classroom educators, or corporate executives; they all are given this scenario:

> *Pretend you are in your kitchen at home. Imagine you are standing in front of the refrigerator. Place a hand on the door handle. Feel the touch of the handle against the palm of your hand. Open the refrigerator door and stand directly in front of the shelves. Feel the cold air as it reaches your bare arms and face. Take a breath and feel that cool air as it enters your nose or mouth.*
>
> *Look directly at the middle shelf. On that shelf is one perfectly shaped, bright yellow lemon. Reach inside the refrigerator and cover the lemon with your hand. Feel the texture of the skin and the cool temperature of the lemon. Lift the lemon from the shelf, move aside and push the door closed.*
>
> *Turn and walk toward the kitchen sink. Open the cabinet door to the side of the sink and take out a small cutting board. Place the lemon on the board. Carefully remove a small knife from the holder on the counter next to the sink. Using one hand to hold the lemon in place, position the knife to carefully slice the lemon in two. As you slice the lemon open, watch several drops of the juice run down the knife blade and settle on the cutting board.*
>
> *Position the knife again, this time to cut one of the lemon halves in half. Place the knife on the cutting board and pick up one of the lemon quarters. Bring the lemon quarter toward your face and smell the pungent aroma. Take a deep breath and draw the scent of the lemon deeper into your lungs. Part your lips as you move the lemon wedge to your mouth. Place the rind of the*

Close your eyes and concentrate all your attention on feeling everything you can imagine you will feel and experience when you actually achieve your goal.

KEY 6

lemon between your teeth...and suck the juice of the lemon flesh into your mouth ...

It never fails. I look around the room and watch as people in the audience pucker in reaction to the *imagined* tart taste of the lemon wedge.

"Why do you all look like that?" I ask in a surprised voice.

"Because I could actually taste it!" someone always answers.

I explain again that our bodies cannot distinguish between a real and an imagined experience. When we imagine any experience or event, our bodies will always produce a response as though the imagined was real.

Have you ever dreamed you were being chased? You awaken and you're out of breath; your heart is racing; you feel as though you've been running for your life! You haven't actually been running. You have been asleep. You only dreamed you were running. But ... your body reacts and manifests the response as though the chase had been real. When you are awake, experiential visualization stimulates your body, mind and emotions to respond in the same way that a dream stimulates those responses when you are asleep.

Through the technique of experiential visualization, the subconscious mind builds success patterns and strengths from an imagined achievement to provide the requirements necessary for the real achievement.

To practice this technique, you must invest three to five minutes a day. If possible, find a place where you can be by yourself, away from any distraction. Close your eyes and concentrate all your attention on feeling everything you can imagine you will feel and experience when you actually achieve your goal.

For example, if your goal is to compete and finish first in a 5K race in your hometown, this is what you might do:

Every day from the date you set this goal, spend at least three to five minutes practicing your experiential visualization. Find a place where you won't be interrupted. Close your eyes and take a few deep breaths to center yourself. Now, experience (imagine, feel) everything you know you will experience and feel when you actually cross that finish line first. If possible, do your experiential visualization exercise more than once a day. Each time you do it, let yourself embrace and enjoy the thrill of your accomplishment. Let yourself go … and feel incredible! The victory is everything you dreamed it would be! Allow yourself to be filled with a sense of pride for all the hard work you've done physically, mentally, emotionally. This moment is yours! You trained hard to get here. You didn't give up; you didn't slack off. You kept on going even when you were tired and your muscles were sore. You earned this victory with your hard work. Breathe in the gratitude you feel for this experience.

In your experiential visualization, live every detail of your victory. Focus and respond mentally, physically and emotionally to stimuli such as:

- Who is waiting for you at the finish line?
- What are you hearing as you cross the finish line?
- How does your body feel?
- What are you thinking?
- What are you wearing?
- What do you see?
- Where are you standing when you accept the trophy?
- How does the trophy feel in your hands; is it cool against the warmth of your skin?
- Is the trophy heavy as you lift it in the air?
- What are you saying as you are interviewed by the media?

As you practice your experiential visualization of this victory, put as much detail and feeling as possible into your effort. Let yourself *feel…*

- Your muscles quivering from exhaustion …
- Your breath coming in short pants …
- A deep flush covering your skin …

- Heat pervading your body ...
- Perspiration dripping from your body and clothing ...
- Your mouth's tight dryness and your thirst for water ...

...and the knowledge that you have won.

Let your experiential visualization go beyond your moment of victory. If your dream is to win the hometown 5K, *go beyond* breaking the ribbon: Experience the feeling of carrying the trophy into your home and placing it where you will see it often. Enjoy the handshakes and hugs of congratulation days later from friends and family who weren't able to be there when you actually crossed the finish line. See yourself (or your mother!) putting the newspaper article about your win in a scrapbook.

There are no limits to how much detail and emotion you can add to this exercise. Like any other kind of exercise, the more you do it, the better you will become at doing it. This is not a time to be modest! In your experiential visualization you are the writer, producer, director and the star. Revel in your role as the winner of your 5K race!

If possible, do your experiential visualization exercise more than once a day. Each time you do it, let yourself embrace and enjoy the thrill of your accomplishment.

Experiential visualization can help you move toward any goal.

Whatever it is that you want to achieve...practice having it happen in your imagination.

During a break in one of our recent teacher trainings, a young woman – let's call her Laurie – came up to me and asked if we could talk privately. She wanted to know if I thought she could use experiential visualization to ensure the success of her new marriage. Laurie said her parents had divorced when she was in high school. Both of her older sisters' marriages had failed. She explained how afraid she had been to accept her husband's (let's call him Eric) proposal

KEY
6

because she had watched too many people whose hearts had been broken by divorce. During our conversation, I learned Laurie and Eric were in their mid-thirties, hoped to have three children, and had been married for only three months.

I told Laurie that practicing experiential visualization would be a great way to protect her marriage and keep it healthy.

"Tell me how!" Laurie said.

I asked Laurie if she and Eric had taken a honeymoon. Laurie's eyes lit up as she explained the perfect week they had spent on the Outer Banks of North Carolina, where they had rented a cottage on the ocean. They agreed the best part of the trip had been sitting in deck chairs at dusk. Laurie said she and Eric promised each other they would go back and stay there again some day. As soon as Laurie told me about the cottage and the sunsets ... I knew how to help her with this exercise!

"Here's my idea," I explained. "Before you fall asleep at night, imagine you and Eric are back at your honeymoon cottage in North Carolina ... celebrating your fiftieth wedding anniversary. Close your eyes and be there 50 years from now. As you sit in those chairs at sunset, you'll be in your eighties. You'll both be 50 years older than you are now, so see yourselves the way you think you'll be at that age. Remember, when you do experiential visualization, you are inside yourself ... looking out at the world as if it were today. In this exercise, the two of you are holding hands. Remember ... your hands are 50 years older than they are today! Your skin won't be as smooth and youthful as it is now. In your experiential visualization you will be two people who have lived and loved together for 50 years.

"Imagine the conversation you are having as the sun sets. You talk about how happy you've been together and how blessed you feel. You speak of your children as the people they are when you've been married five decades. You reminisce about your grandchildren and even your great-grandchildren – about the wonderful holidays

> **In addition to accelerating you toward your goal, experiential visualization is an oasis of joy you can access every day of your life.**

KEY 6

when they were growing up.

"Laurie, just put all your feelings of happiness and gratitude into this imagined conversation. Share the dreams you and Eric planned when you stayed at the cottage 50 years earlier. Talk about the big moments during those 50 years … like buying your first home, becoming grandparents for the first time. Share memories of the little day-to-day details, too."

The rest of the class was coming back into the room after our break. I told Laurie we could talk again at the end of the day or wait until tomorrow after she had had the chance to give her experiential visualization a try.

That next day, we didn't have the chance to talk again. It was the following week on the last day of the class before we were able to catch up.

"You won't believe how this is working!" Laurie told me. "After we talked last week, I told Eric what you suggested. He said he'd never heard of experiential visualization, but thought it sounded like something we should do together. Before we go to sleep, we hold hands and pretend we're sitting in those deck chairs on the beach 50 years from now. We talk about all the things you suggested and lots more! This is so much fun! This morning, Eric told me to say thank you from him. He said he thinks this is the best idea ever!"

Whether your goal is to have a happy marriage, find the perfect job, win a 5K, or be the best parent on the planet, use your imagination through the technique of experiential visualization to help you achieve your desire. In addition to accelerating you toward your goal, experiential visualization is an oasis of joy you can access every day of your life. It's a vacation from all the have-to-dos of the day.

Practicing the full emotional feeling of achievement is the most important part of any experiential visualization. The more you allow yourself to feel the utter satisfaction, joy, gratitude, self-esteem and pride of the accomplished goal, the more fuel you add to the power of your imagination.

How does Acting As If work?

Acting As If helps you develop the personal characteristics needed for achieving a goal and becoming the person you want to be.

This technique is every bit as enjoyable as experiential visualization. It is also equally easy to learn. To use the technique of Acting As If, you need to consider the characteristics and habits you think might be required to reach a particular goal and those you believe are necessary to becoming the person you want to be. Talk to people you trust and explain what you want to accomplish. Ask for their advice and add it to what you have already considered.

For example: If your goal is to become the top salesperson in your company, what qualities would you need to possess? Your list might look like this:

- excellent product knowledge
- active listener
- skilled negotiator
- respectful of others' time
- well-spoken and succinct
- patient, persistent, persuasive
- organized
- goal-oriented

KEY 6

You could add other qualities to this list ... but this is a start. To become the top salesperson in your company, you start Acting As If you already possess and express these qualities. Act As If you have excellent product knowledge, are an active listener, are a skilled negotiator, etc. By Acting As If you already *are* all these things, you *automatically* begin to express these characteristics, and before you know it, you have *become* the person you want to be.

Using your imagination to Act As If is energizing to your body, mind and emotions. It challenges your mind and body to work in a higher, faster, more powerful gear. Acting As If works quickly and never fails. When you Act As If you already are the person you want to be, you become more than you have ever been before. The celebrated actor Cary Grant once said, "I pretended to be somebody I wanted to be, and finally I became that person. Or he became me."

"Imagination is everything! It is a preview of life's coming attractions." – Albert Einstein

Imagination clearly fascinated the great scientist, who also said, "Logic will get you from A to B. Imagination will take you everywhere."

The first time I had a front-row seat to how imagination can fuel a dream (aka, goal) was when I watched my daughter use it to achieve something very important to her when she was just eleven years old.

> **It challenges your mind and body to work in a higher, faster, more powerful gear. Acting As If works quickly and never fails.**

KEY 6

MARIE, THE LITTLE CHEERLEADER
by Judy Zerafa

When my daughter was in the sixth grade, she suffered from low self-confidence. Today, I can see why. I was the poster child for low self-confidence. My daughter was simply imitating me. She believed everyone was more talented, better-looking, luckier, smarter than she was.

I realized how serious low self-confidence could be after attending a seminar in the autumn of the year Marie entered sixth grade. As a single mom without an education, I was trying to improve myself in order to improve all our lives. It was shortly after that seminar that I began to see how crippling my example had become to my children. Especially Marie, who was the eldest. I watched her become more withdrawn and unhappy each day. She seemed particularly sad one evening. I knew we had to talk. I wanted to see if there was anything I could do to help her.

After tucking the younger two children in bed, I asked Marie to come and sit with me in the living room. We walked in; she sat at one end of the sofa and I sat at the other. I said, "I know it's late, and you're tired but I need you to tell me what's making you so sad." She didn't answer. I finally said, "We're not going to bed until you tell me what's going on." I waited. She still didn't answer. "Okay, then I guess we'll just sit here all night. I love you and I want to help, but I can't if I don't know what's wrong."

Marie said something, but she said it so quietly I was sure I had misunderstood. I thought she said, "I can't be a cheerleader."

I moved closer to her and asked her to tell me again. I hadn't misunderstood. She said, "I can't be a cheerleader."

I didn't understand the words she was saying ... but I did understand the tears welling up in her eyes. "What does your not being able to be a cheerleader have to do with anything?" I asked.

Marie slumped against the cushions and said, "I knew you wouldn't understand."

"Help me to understand."

Marie looked away for a few seconds. When she turned toward me she explained the principal had announced that the school was going to finally have a full athletic program. They were even going to have a cheerleading squad.

I still didn't understand. I waited for her to explain further.

"Mom, I really want to be a cheerleader."

"Marie, that's great! So ... why are you acting so unhappy?"

Marie shook her head and said, "I knew you wouldn't understand. That's why I don't want to talk about it."

"What don't I understand?" I asked with exasperation.

The tears that had been forming in the corners of her eyes spilled over and slid slowly down her cheeks. "It's just a stupid dream, mom. No one is going to vote for me."

I looked at the sadness on Marie's face and the defeat underscored by her posture. I had a strange out-of-body experience as I sat beside my daughter. I could feel myself doing backward somersaults. When I landed ... I was eleven years old again. I knew exactly how my daughter was feeling. I had lived my whole life feeling that way: always on the outside looking in. Never good enough. I saw my life flash in front of me. Everything I was, everything I had ... was the result of lack of confidence. My daughter was headed down that very same path ...

> **I saw my life flash in front of me. Everything I was, everything I had ... was the result of lack of confidence. My daughter was headed down that very same path.**

Moving closer to Marie, I put my arms around her. I kissed the top of her head and held her while she cried. When she stopped, I turned her face toward me and asked, "How important is this cheerleading thing to you?"

She answered softly, "I don't think I ever wanted

KEY

6

anything more."

I thought about what I'd been doing to improve my own life ... based on what I'd recently learned about the power of imagination. I reached for a tissue and wiped the tears from Marie's eyes.

"I have an idea," I told her. "I'm going to teach you something I've been using. I can't promise this will guarantee that you get chosen to be on the cheerleading squad, but it's the best advice I have." I explained about imagination and learning to Act As If. I told Marie to start telling herself she was a cheerleader. I told her to practice by saying it out loud...to me.

After several tries, the best Marie could do was barely above a whisper. I looked at the clock and it was late! We were both going to be tired the next day!

"Okay, kiddo," I told her. "Let's call it a night and I'll explain the rest tomorrow. How much time do you have between now and tryouts?"

"Six weeks."

We had a lot of work to do...

> **I thought about what I'd been doing to improve my own life ... based on what I'd recently learned about the power of imagination.**

I waited for Marie to get ready for bed. We said our prayers together and I tucked her in. We whispered so we wouldn't wake her little sister, sleeping quietly in the same room. I sat on the bed next to Marie and said, "I know it's late, but there's one more thing I need to tell you before you fall asleep. I want you to close your eyes and imagine you really are a cheerleader. I want you to experience inside yourself all the feelings you would have if you actually were a cheerleader."

Marie whispered, "I'm not sure I understand."

"Close your eyes. Take a deep, relaxing breath. Get centered inside yourself. You're wearing a cheerleading uniform. You are in the school gym, standing in front of the bleachers. In front of you are your classmates, their parents and friends from other schools. The basketball team is on the court behind you. Your job is to cheer the team to victory! It's noisy! Everyone is excited! The team is winning! You are yelling at the top of your voice!

"Be inside yourself," I continued. "Don't close your eyes and pretend you're watching yourself on a monitor. Be inside yourself, feeling all those exciting feelings! Hearing all the noise. Being part of the cheerleading squad!"

"Okay," Marie responded. "I think I understand."

"Alright, then. Keep doing this for a few minutes before you fall asleep," I said as I kissed her forehead. I walked to the door and quietly turned out the light ... but not before I took one last look at Marie's sweet face. Her eyes were tightly closed ... and the beginning of a smile tugged at her lips. "Oh yes!" I told myself. "She is doing it right!"

I set my alarm a few minutes earlier than usual. When it rang, I tiptoed into the girls' room and sat on the edge of Marie's bed. I touched her shoulder to wake her. When she opened her eyes, I whispered, "Before you get out of bed, there's one more thing I need to tell you." Marie rubbed her eyes and sat up against the pillows. "When you get dressed, *pretend* you're putting on your cheerleading uniform. Feel the knit of that sweater as you pull it over your head and put your arms in the sleeves. It has your name across the front and the school name across the back. When you put on your skirt, remember it is your cheerleading uniform skirt. You need to imagine you are wearing this all day today."

Marie scooted to the edge of the bed, her eyes as big as saucers. "Mom, do I have to tell anybody what I am doing?" she asked with concern.

"No!" I answered with excitement and encouragement.. "That's the best part! You're going to do all of this using your imagination. Wait until you see how it makes you feel!"

When everyone was up, dressed and ready, I drove my children to school. I pulled into the student drop-off area and got out of the car to give everyone a hug. "Remember, you're wearing a cheerleading uniform today," I whispered to Marie.

I was in the kitchen when my children got home from school that afternoon. Ted and Mary came through the door first. When Marie walked into the kitchen, I whirled around and asked, "Who are you?"

Marie stared at me, then said, "You are so weird."

"Weird or not," I asked her again, "who are you?"

It took a couple of seconds for her to figure out the game. "I'm a cheerleader," she said, with just a tad more enthusiasm than the night before.

For the next six weeks, every time she and I were alone, I would look at her and ask, "Who are you?"

As the weeks went by, Marie would answer, "I'm a cheerleader!" Each time, her answer was more enthusiastic.

I reminded her to do her experiential visualization exercise each night as I tucked her in. When I awakened her for school, I would say, "Wear that cheerleading uniform with pride today, young lady!"

Six weeks passed quickly. Marie practiced the cheerleading routines every day. She told me she Acted As If all the time ... and did her experiential visualization every night.

And finally ... it was the BIG day. When I pulled into the student drop-off area, I looked over and saw a mixture of excitement and fear in Marie's eyes. I reached over to touch her and told her she would be great. I gave her change and asked her to be sure to call me as soon as the tryouts were over.

As my three little troopers filed through the school door, I sat in my car and just shook from nerves. "Oh, my gosh, what am I going to do if she doesn't make it!" I thought "She will be devastated. She will go back to being so sad ... and things will be worse than they've ever been."

I knew what I had to do. I did what any loving parent would

do: I made a deal with God. "If you let her have this," I prayed, "I'll never ask for anything else as long as I live."

I'm older now ... and maybe wiser. As I wrote that last paragraph, I could imagine God rolling His eyes at my promise and laughing out loud. He knew I'd be back ... asking for many more favors for all my children ... because that's what parents do.

It took forever for the day to move to late afternoon. At 4:00, the phone rang. I knew it was Marie. The palm of my hand was so wet with sweat I had trouble lifting the receiver to my ear. When it was half-way there, I heard her voice scream, "Mom, I didn't just make the squad, I'm the captain!"

My hand shook as I pressed the receiver more firmly to my ear. "Oh Marie! I'm so proud of you! We're going to have such a celebration tonight!"

On my way home from work, I made a quick stop at the store and bought hot dogs, cupcakes, and all the things you need to celebrate something this wonderful.

Her little brother and sister were proud and wanted to take pictures. We put candles on the cupcakes and sang our version of congratulations to the Happy Birthday tune. We had a perfect family evening. I felt like Marie's success was a sign for all of us.

> **She told me she Acted As If all the time ... and did her experiential visualization every night.**

When the little ones were tucked in their beds, I put my arm around Marie and we walked together into the living room. "We need to talk," I said.

We sat close together, as we had on that night six weeks earlier. "I'm so proud of you," I told my daughter. "I know that what you learned to do with your imagination will help you with anything you ever want to achieve in the future. Experiential visualization and Acting As If will always give you an extra advantage when you're working toward a goal. What I want to do tonight

KEY 6

is make sure you understand how your imagination helped you achieve something you didn't believe you could do.

"To make sure you do understand how you became a cheerleader, I want you to start at the beginning and tell me how you went from not thinking you could even try out … to being voted captain of the squad."

Marie said, "I don't know what you want me to say."

"Talk to me about what happened. Tell me when and where you could see yourself changing."

Marie explained that the first day she went to school in her pretend uniform she was in health class when her teacher asked for a volunteer to answer a question. Marie said she did what she always had done when any teacher called for a volunteer: She closed her eyes and scooted down in her chair to try and make herself invisible. She explained that she must have scooted with more enthusiasm than usual because she ended up on the floor. After everyone stopped laughing, Marie remembered she was wearing her cheerleading uniform. She said she felt like she needed to at least try to answer the question. She raised her hand; the teacher called on her but Marie didn't get the answer right. She admitted that was the first time she had ever volunteered to try and answer a question since she had started school.

> "What I want to do tonight is make sure you understand how your imagination helped you achieve something you didn't believe you could do."

I asked Marie if she had noticed all of her grades had improved over this marking period. I pointed out how much more time she was putting into her homework every evening, "I'm wondering if you've been trying harder because you thought you might want to participate more in class because you were Acting As If."

"I didn't think of it exactly like that," Marie answered, "but I know that's what I was doing."

"Tell me other things you noticed because you were Acting

As If."

"I made myself start talking to kids I didn't know." Marie was so excited as she explained what had happened. "Mom, you never told us how easy it is to make friends! The secret is you just ask them questions about themselves! When you do that, everyone wants to talk to you! Between classes I would ask, 'How did you do on the math test?' 'Are you going to sign up for the science fair?'"

I told her she was very wise. "Tell me more," I encouraged.

"Well, here's the biggest thing: Do you remember two weeks ago when I asked if I could stay after class to work on a project?"

I nodded my confirmation.

"You said yes. That was the day the boys had tryouts for track team. I finished my project in class early, so I went in the gym to wait for you. Danny, from my class, was there. I asked why he wasn't outside trying out. Well, he said he wasn't going to try out. I couldn't understand why … because Danny has always been a good runner. I could see, the way he was acting, he was worried about not making the team and then being embarrassed.

"Mom! I told him he had to try. I explained our school needed him because he was a good runner. He shook his head. He wasn't going to try out. I kept telling him he was a good runner and had to try."

Marie said Danny kept saying, "What if I go out there and I don't make it? I don't want everyone laughing at me. I'm not going to do it." And that she kept saying, "Danny, you've been one of the fastest runners in the whole school since first grade! You have to try out! This is the first year our school has sports teams, Danny. You need to do this!" Marie paused for breath.

"Mom, he kept shaking his head sideways, telling me he wasn't going to try out. I kept telling him he could make the team if he tried. All of a sudden, he stopped shaking his head. We talked a little longer, and he started shaking his head yes.

"You need to get out there NOW, I told him. You CAN do this. You're good!

"Mom, when Danny stood up and headed across the gym floor ... I knew he was going to go out and try. I felt so good! I didn't need anyone to tell me I was a cheerleader. I felt like I really was one!"

I could see with my own eyes how much Marie had changed. It had been only six weeks, but she even looked different.

My daughter and I sat there looking at each other for what seemed like a long time as we both realized what had happened. "Marie, I'm so proud of you. Can you see that whether or not you had been chosen to be on the cheerleading squad, you've become a real cheerleader? By Acting As If you *were* a cheerleader, you *became* a cheerleader. You *became* a person who cheers others on ... and helps them see their worth."

Marie absolutely glowed! "Just think about how sad you were six weeks ago. You didn't see your own ability. You were afraid to try. You felt alone. Now look at you!"

"I just know I've never felt this good," Marie said with a smile I'll always remember.

"There will be a lot of things you want to accomplish during your life," I promised my daughter. "You will probably have many goals. I hope you always remember to use your imagination whenever you set a goal ... no matter how big or small that goal might seem.

"I'm not going to tell you that you will reach every single goal you ever set for yourself. I'm not sure I know anyone who ever has. Just remember how much fun you've had with experiential visualization. It really does help as you're working on a goal. And, keep Acting As If you are the person you want to be ... because here's the magical part: **By Acting As If you are the person you want to be ... you become more than you've ever been before.**"

Marie, The Little Cheerleader: Key Connections

Marie's success in using her imagination helped her have the best school year she had ever had. I've watched her use experiential visualization and Acting As If to achieve so many of her dreams!

My daughter is out of school now. She's all grown up with children of her own.

I sat in the back of a room one evening recently and listened to Marie present a portion of a seminar for business colleagues. She stressed the importance of creative imagination, explaining how she had used experiential visualization and Acting As If to achieve goals she'd set as a student, in her career, as a parent ... and most recently, in her goal of overcoming cancer.

My daughter is my hero.

Imagination really *is* everything ...

> **I could see with my own eyes how much Marie had changed. It had been only six weeks, but she even looked different.**

What is it that *YOU* want?

- a stronger family?
- greater health and better fitness?
- a promotion in your job/career?
- being a better parent, spouse, friend, employer/employee?
- better financial opportunities?

Your imagination has the power to help you achieve these, or any other, worthy goals.

FACTS TO REMEMBER

- The techniques of experiential visualization and Acting As If strengthen and expand the power of creative imagination.
- When experiential visualization and Acting As If are practiced with a positive attitude, applied to increasing a personal talent or ability, supported by self-enhancing habits, wise choices and attached to a goal...creative imagination becomes powerful beyond belief.

KEY 6

Family Activities

We hope you have fun teaching your children the Seven Keys to Success along *Your Path To An EASIER & BETTER Life*. Remember, children learn most readily by example. As a parent, your example is the most powerful example in their lives. You can be sure your child is watching and learning. The more you work to incorporate the Seven Keys into your life, the greater the chances are that your children will embrace and adopt them into their lives.

Below are suggestions for family activities that will help you develop creative imagination individually and as a family.

1. As the leader for this session (or the family leader), have all family members open their notebooks to the first blank page and write "Key 6 – Activities" at the top of the page.

2. Have each person go back to his or her notes for Key 5 and, in turn, share with everyone else the personal goal he or she would like to achieve.

> **Encourage everyone to choose what he or she wants to be responsible for in contributing toward this goal.**

3. Once everyone has had the chance to share, take turns again. This time, each individual will give his or her ideas on what experiential visualization will be used *toward* that individual's goal. Make sure all family members create their individual visualization to embrace the completed achievement. If there is any doubt about what this means, go back in this Key and refer to the example of winning a 5K race in your hometown. The details of this win are not only the moments experienced after accepting the trophy, but also the feelings experienced days later as well-wishers continue to extend congratulations. There is also the example of Laurie, the teacher, and her experiential visualization of a lasting, successful marriage.

As each person explains what experiential visualization he or she will use, go around the room and have everyone add ideas to help expand and intensify this exercise for the person who will be practicing it.

If a child is too young to take notes, encourage everyone else to help with appropriate reminders. This is a great bedtime strategy for little ones.

4. Go around the table once more, taking turns with ideas for Acting As If for each person's goal. Encourage note-taking.

5. Remind everyone to catch-and-comment when he or she sees family members Acting As If.

6. In Key 5, you chose a family goal. For this activity, discuss creating a family experiential visualization. This will be an exercise you practice whenever you have three to five minutes together to *experience* your family goal as though it has already been achieved.

For example, if your goal is to adopt a family pet, your experiential visualization might be three to five minutes of enthusiastic memory-sharing of fun times with your pet. Each family member will share his or her thoughts, feelings and comments about the experience. You might pretend it is two or three years into the future, and you're all talking about what a great decision you made because this pet has been so perfect for each of you.

7. Ask everyone to play Act As If for one of your family goals. This family goal can be the same as the one you are doing with your family's experiential visualization exercise, or it can be a different one.

If one of your family goals is to keep your home clean and in good repair, have everyone start Acting As If your home is clean and in repair. Each person will start to Act As If by taking responsibility toward some part of this goal. Encourage everyone to choose what he or she wants to be responsible for in contributing toward this goal. As each of you plays your part of Acting As If, you are all making sure your home *stays* clean and in good repair.

8. Ask everyone to turn to the next blank page in the notebook. Have everyone write his or her personal goal from Key 5 at the top of this page. Beneath the goal, write the following statements along the left side of the page, skipping a line between each statement:

I am
I wonder
I hear
I see

I am
I pretend
I feel
I touch
I am
I understand
I say
I dream
I try

I am

On every line that starts with *I am*, ask everyone to write his or her full name. On the other lines, ask them to write what *immediately comes to mind after each phrase in connection to the goal they have written at the top of the page*. Encourage everyone to write his or her reaction or feeling to each phrase spontaneously.

When everyone has finished, take turns reading what each of you has written.

9. Have everyone go to the next blank page and write his or her goal at the top again. Along the left side of the page write the follow-

ing, leaving a line between each phrase:
I am
I wonder
I hear
I see
I want

I am
I pretend
I feel
I touch

I am
I understand
I say
I dream
I try
I do

I am

Just as in the first part of this exercise, ask family members to write their full name each time they come to the phrase that starts with I am.

Following all the other phrases, have everyone write his or her response *as though he or she has already achieved this goal.*

When everyone has finished, take turns reading. Encourage everyone to listen to the difference between the feelings and responses from the first list ... and those from the second. **This activity encourages everyone to focus on the feelings of the accomplished goal when creating his or her experiential visualization ... and when practicing Acting As If.**

This exercise was created by Yolanda Ortega, Assistant Principal at Trevista at Horace Mann, an ECE-8 School in Denver Public Schools of Colorado. Ms. Ortega uses this exercise to help her students get in touch with their feelings relative to their goals. She

explains how emotional energy helps create powerful experiential visualizations and Act As If behaviors. I did this exercise with her students one day and was surprised to see how much it adds to these two techniques!

Between now and the next time you have a family session:

Encourage each family member to continue looking for changes in one's self and other family members ... and comment on these! By making a commitment to Act As If you are who you want to be as individuals, and who you want to be as a family team ... you will see positive results. By cheering each other's victories and encouraging each other through challenge, you will continue making your lives better in every way.

Congratulations! You have one more Key to go!

KEY

6

PERSISTENCE

A Deliberate Decision to Keep Trying Until Success Is Achieved

Fundamentals

- All successful people are persistent.
- Everyone is capable of persistence.

What is persistence?

According to the Merriam-Webster Dictionary, "Persistence is the action, or fact, of persisting."

Your Path To An EASIER & BETTER Life describes *persistence* as the determination to continue in spite of difficulty or challenges. Persistence is the line that separates success from failure.

Why is it important to be persistent?

In the Introduction, I explain how I discovered the Seven Keys to Success through interviews with 35 recipients of the Horatio Alger Award. All 35 award recipients epitomized success in their fields of endeavor. All 35 believed a positive attitude and persistence were fundamental to success, regardless of how success might be defined personally.

Most of us come to realize that achieving anything important rarely happens on our first try. Our dreams and significant goals take effort. The bigger our goals, the more effort they require. Education is a good example of this. Most of us don't get through school without putting effort into learning. Not many of us find love on the first try.

KEY 7

We don't become skilled at any sport the first time we play.

No baseball player has ever been signed to a professional team after playing only one game. It takes *years* of practice and *years* of winning and losing games before a player is even considered by the pro teams. Professional athletes understand that the difference between where they started and where they are today is about *never giving up.* Never!

Persistence is not just the winning ticket in sports; it is the winning ticket in every human endeavor. The reason we can walk, recite the alphabet, or ride a bike is because we kept on trying until we were able to do so. *We developed persistence. We understood that giving up was not an option.*

Persistence is the determination to try again…no matter how many times you fail. Try … Fail … Try … Fail … Try again. And fail again. Persistence is what made Thomas Edison try and fail 4,999 times before he succeeded in inventing a working light bulb.

Persistence is what made J.K. Rowling keep writing and keep sending her stories to publishers even though her work was rejected time after time. Rowling wanted to inspire children, to help readers experience the power of their own imaginations through her story-telling. She was a single mother living on welfare when she began writing her Harry Potter stories in 1990. Despite the challenges in her life and the rejection of publishers who told her no one would read what she wrote, J.K. Rowling refused to give up. Today, Rowling is the most famous children's writer of all time. She has inspired people of every age to connect, or reconnect, to reading; she has ignited imaginations around the world. She has also become the wealthiest author who has ever lived.

> **Persistence is developed through the investment of time and effort into something that is important to us.**

How does a person develop persistence?

Persistence is developed through the investment of time and effort into something that is important to us. The *decision* to persist is one of the best decisions we can ever make. It is a gift we give our self.

When I first began studying the subject of success, I read an article by Earl Nightingale. The celebrated radio broadcaster explained that anyone can become an expert within a particular area of interest through the investment of one hour a day for three years. A one-hour a day investment over three years equals 1,095 hours of effort. Can you imagine what you can learn with that many hours of study? Can you imagine what you could accomplish with that many hours of practice?

Just imagine how much math you can learn in 1,095 hours! Or how very knowledgeable you can become about architecture, ancient cultures, literature, graphic arts, geography, science, technology or finance! What if you invested an hour a day for three years practicing a musical instrument? Learning to cook? Running? Playing basketball? Hockey? Tennis? Golf? Football? Learning to act? Singing? Dancing? Learning to sculpt?

Investing time and effort in something that interests us is the best investment we can ever make. An investment in our self will always bring its own reward.

Opportunities to reinforce the benefits of persistence with your child are everywhere! When you watch a sports competition with your son or daughter, use that opportunity to talk about how much work it takes to develop the ability to play the game you are watching together. When you visit the doctor's office, talk about how many years of study and training it takes to become a physician. When you see a piece of sculpture or a picture in a place of honor, talk about what hard work you imagine it must have taken before the artist's work was exhibited.

Key 7, PERSISTENCE, is the fuel, converted from our hard work and effort, that drives us to succeed.

How many designs were developed ... and then scrapped ... before the car your family drives was produced? How many different recipes were put together and then tested before the cake mix you bought at the grocery store was perfected and packaged? How much time did it take before you could type on a keyboard without looking at the keys?

Everywhere you look, there are examples of *persistence*!

Practice does make perfect!

I was just beginning to practice the Seven Keys to Success in my own life as I watched Scott Hamilton win the Olympic Gold Medal in figure skating one night in February years ago. I knew as I watched that I was witnessing the result of incredible persistence.

Several years later, I had the privilege of meeting Scott and spending a week working with him on a project.

I had never heard Scott's name before the night he won his Olympic Gold Medal. I became an instant fan. From that night on, I watched every television interview he ever did. I read every story in every magazine and newspaper about this incredible athlete. I was beyond impressed by the challenges Scott Hamilton had faced at every step of his journey toward becoming the first figure skater in Olympic history to ever receive a perfect score. He overcame illness, physical injuries, personal setbacks, learning disorders, and even the death of his mother when he was in his early teens. When we met, I joked with Scott about my knowing more about him than any of his other fans. I was certain there was no one in the world who had followed his career with as much respect and admiration as I had. I told him I used the story of his persistence to end the speeches I gave to students, teachers and families.

As we finished our project and were saying goodbye, Scott asked if I would include a message from him to my future audiences. "When you tell my story, be sure to explain there's no *secret* to success. Tell everyone success is a simple formula: 2 parts talent + 98 parts work = success."

For the past 18 years, I have included Scott's important message in every speech I've given.

Persistence connects the Keys to Success

We are each born with specific talents and abilities. Key 2 shows us how to discover our unique talents and abilities. Keys 1, 3, 4, 5 and 6 provide the strategies for developing these gifts. Key 7, PERSISTENCE, is the fuel, converted from our hard work and effort, that drives us to success. Without the fuel of hard work and effort, it is impossible to succeed.

FACTS TO REMEMBER

- Everyone is capable of success. ("Everyone" includes you, your child, and your family team.)
- Success is achieved through a very simple formula:

  2 parts talent + 98 parts hard work = SUCCESS.
- Persistence is the fuel created by your hard work.

Family Activities

We hope you have fun teaching your children the Seven Keys to Success along *Your Path To An EASIER & BETTER Life*. Remember, children learn most readily by example. As a parent, your example is the most powerful example in their lives. You can be sure your child is watching and learning. The more you work to incorporate the Seven Keys into your life, the greater the chances are that your children will embrace and adopt them into their lives.

Below are suggestions for family activities that will help you develop persistence individually and as a family.

1. Have all family members open their notebooks to the first blank page and write "Key 7 – Activities" at the top of the page.

2. Take turns explaining what *persistence* means. Encourage everyone to take notes to use later as reminders.

3. Go around the table and have each person give an example of someone he or she believes has developed persistence. This person can be someone known to family members; it can be someone they

don't personally know, but who is thought to have persistence; or a character in a book or movie. *The point of this activity is to make sure everyone in your family group understands what persistence looks like in action.*

4. It is much easier to keep trying, to keep working toward a goal, when you have the support of others. Your family members can... and should...become the greatest support to each other. During the process of learning the Keys to Success on *Your Path To An EASIER & BETTER Life*, you have shared your personal and family goals in the Activities. You know what the other members of your family are working to achieve.

In this activity, take turns going around the table and *ask for the support* you want from each family member individually. Encourage everyone to be brave and honest as he or she makes the request.

For example, there may be a family member who isn't comfortable being hugged in public. If the goal that person is working on involves something that would be practiced in public – like playing a sport – that person might ask not to be hugged in front of his or her classmates or friends. They may ask for a thumbs-up, a high-five, a fist-bump or some other sign of encouragement or support. Others may be okay with hugs in public, but have other areas of discomfort. *Encourage everyone in your family to ask for what he or she needs and give what each is asked to give.*

Sometimes, we don't know what we want from others. If someone in your family isn't sure of how he or she wants to receive encouragement and support from other family members, brainstorm ideas as a team. We all have instincts about what makes us feel comfortable. This is a perfect time to explore what you need from each other. With patience and honest communication, you will discover the way to encourage and support each other. This activity could turn out to be the most important thing you take away from the entire family session experience.

KEY
7

A Positive Attitude • Belief in One's Self • Positive Habits
Wise Choices • Setting and Achieving Goals
Using Creative Imagination • Persistence

An Unforeseen Connection

Serendipity has played a significant part in the development of the Seven Keys to Success Program. From the moment this journey began, there have been many "coincidences" that moved this message forward. Several years ago, Squire Rushnell, a former executive at ABC, wrote a book about coincidences titled *When God Winks at You*. In his book, Rushnell coined the word *godwinks* to explain that these seemingly impossible coincidences that deliver joy and magic to us are messages from God reminding us that He cares about the details of our lives. I love that book! And the word godwink has become part of my everyday vocabulary.

As I began writing this book, the GO FOR IT! Institute received a stunning godwink. We learned that our Seven Keys to Success, discovered through another coincidence decades ago, then developed through years of passion and effort, had been validated by nearly three decades of professional, scientific research. Quality Evaluation Designs, a company that provides educational research, evaluation and policy, issued a white paper in 2010 entitled "The Psychological Foundations of the Seven Keys to Success." This in-depth report by Martin L. Tombari, Ph.D., and Gary Lichtenstein, Ed.D., established a solid link between the Seven Keys to Success and the School of Positive Psychology. Tombari and Lichtenstein, educational psychology specialists, identified three specific methodologies of the School's applied research and noted: "These three together constitute the foundation of the Positive Psychology movement as well as the theoretical underpinnings of the Seven Keys to Success."

As the message of the Seven Keys to Success was evolving into a school program in the 1980s, a group of child psychologists and researchers began to explore a new direction in their field. For over 50 years, psychoanalytical theory and practice had been driven by the Freudian and Behaviorist schools, which focused on maladaptive manifestations in families and children. In the 1990s, a new perspective in psychology turned its focus in the opposite direction. The Positive Psychology movement began asking, "What makes people – adults, children, families – successful, in school and in society?" In 1999, Dr. Mihaly Csikszentmihalyi at California's Claremont Graduate University founded the Quality of Life Research Center (QLRC) to study "positive psychology," that is, human strengths such as optimism, creativity, intrinsic motivation, and responsibility. Claremont Graduate University began offering Ph.D. and M.A. concentrations focused on the Science of Positive Psychology. The success of this movement grew into an established school of thought that has evolved and been embraced in theory and practice around the world.

> **The in-depth report established a solid link between the GO FOR IT! Seven Keys to Success and the School of Positive Psychology.**

Connecting School of Positive Psychology and Seven Keys to Success

- **SDT connects to Key 2 – Belief in One's Self and Key 7 – Persistence**

The Self-Determination Theory (SDT) within the Positive Psychology movement emphatically expresses that we are born "predisposed toward wanting to succeed, and as a result have innate needs, which, if nurtured, will lead to success." According to University of Rochester researchers who have been testing SDT in the field and in the laboratory for 30 years, these "innate needs" are "competence, relatedness and autonomy."

Seven Keys to Success Key 2 (Belief In One's Self) provides the strategies for uncovering and developing the talents and abilities that comprise our human potential. Children at the early elementary school level are able to use these strategies to begin discovering their personal treasure and move in the direction of personal fulfillment and purpose.

The "need for competence" expressed by SDT is our motivation to succeed at tasks, meet challenges and achieve goals. The "need for autonomy" is our desire for choice over what we do and how we do it. The "need for relatedness" is our hunger for mutual trust and reliance in the context of social cooperation. These innate needs are connected to instinctive drives to satisfy them.

Persistence is a fundamental component of the Self-Determination Theory developed by Richard Ryan and Edward Deci of the University of Rochester. SDT urges children to persist in their goal-seeking strategies, and to encourage themselves and each other to keep trying in the face of adversity or challenge.

Seven Keys to Success Key 7 – Persistence is a personal trait that develops naturally with the practice of the previous six keys in the Seven Keys to Success Program. Just as self-esteem flows naturally from self-confidence, persistence is the natural outcome of practicing a positive attitude, belief in one's self, positive habits, wise choices, goal setting, and imagination.

> **Seligman's research supports the belief that the habit of optimistic styles of thinking can be acquired and become habitual.**

SDT concludes that when adults provide a *fulfilling environment*, children not only develop self-determination, engagement, initiative and self-confidence, but go on to build a wide range of strategies to achieve success. They see themselves as "agents of their success."

Through Keys 2 and 7, Seven Keys to Success connects the *theory* of Self-Determination to the *strategies* for uncovering and developing the specific talents and abilities that comprise the potential of an individual and the conscious determination to achieve and succeed.

- **LOT connects to Key 1 – A Positive Attitude and Key 3 – Positive Habits**

Learned Optimism Theory (LOT) research explains that optimism and pessimism are learned and habitual, and they are developed from nurture rather than nature.

For most of the 20th century, Freudian and Behaviorist schools taught that certain behaviors occur because of forces beyond our control. Drs. Tombari and Lichtenstein explain that in the 1990s "cognitive psychologists led by Aaron Beck, Albert Ellis and Martin Seligman showed that people develop habits of thinking about their successes and failures. These are referred to as "explanatory styles." People use habits of thinking to explain the reasons for what happens to them. Tombari and Lichtenstein cite the old country-song refrain, "I guess we're just gonna be who we're gonna be" as a negative explanatory style that blocks well-being in adults and children.

Seven Keys to Success Key 3 – Positive Habits explains how all habits, both positive and negative, are formed. This Key teaches how to erase habits that hold us back and replace them with habits that move us forward. Key 3 also emphasizes the power of our words, and the implied messages of our body language and attitude, in sponsoring habits within the subconscious of others … particularly our children.

The leading researcher in explanatory styles, Martin Seligman at the University of Pennsylvania, has shown through numerous large-scale longitudinal-research programs that explanatory styles are learned and can be unlearned. Seligman's research supports the belief that the habit of optimistic styles of thinking can be acquired and become habitual. He believes the explanatory style takes root in a child around age seven.

LOT contends that children instinctively want to believe they are efficient, that they are active self-change agents, capable of success. Children, however, are sadly vulnerable to adults' modeling of negative explanatory styles. Children need adults who have formed the habit of an optimistic explanatory style to model and nurture this habit for them.

Seven Keys to Success Keys 1 and 3 are closely aligned to Seligman's research and methods for teaching optimism strategies. Tombari and Lichtenstein conclude that "learning an 'optimistic explanatory style' (Seligman's language) and 'learning a positive attitude' (language of Seven Keys to Success curriculum) refer to identical cognitive processes."

Through two decades of teaching the strategies for developing and maintaining a positive attitude (Key 1), and replacing negative habits with positive habits (Key 3), the Seven Keys to Success Program has proven that children as young as three are capable of learning these life skills. Our observation, supported by the anecdotal evidence of school administrators, classroom teachers and parents, reinforces our belief that adult role-modeling of positive attitude and positive habits is the best way to teach these essential life skills. Positive Psychology shares this perspective.

- **SRL connects to Key 4 – Wise Choices, Key 5 – Setting and Achieving Goals, and Key 6 – Using Creative Imagination**

Cognitive psychologist Barry Zimmerman with the City University of New York began working out the basic assumptions of Self-Regulated Learning (SRL) in the 1980s. SRL promotes a take-charge belief system in which children acquire knowledge and skills on their own, enhancing their beliefs that they can help themselves and need not rely on adults. Zimmerman's question was, "How do we get children to become responsible for their own learning?" His research provided this answer: Within the framework of choice-making, goal-setting and self-evaluation. Zimmerman coined the term self-efficacy for the confidence children have about their potential to learn skills and perform them proficiently. Step Two in SRL requires children/students to carry out strategies such as completing homework, checking their own work, keeping records, comparing achievements to goals, self-praise and memorizing. Step Three asks adults/teachers to model the desired behaviors created by these strategies for their children/students.

Seven Keys to Success Key 4 teaches adults and children to decide in advance how they want their lives to look at the end of the day, what result they want to enjoy from a specific effort. In the words of

Drs. Tombari and Lichtenstein: "Key 4 lessons encourage children ... to make the proactive choices that are necessary to get the desired result. Good choices make good actions and positive results follow ... SRL strategies reflect proactive choices that students make about how best to reach their goals ..."

SRL also stresses the importance of having children set goals and define strategies for achieving these goals. The SRL methods include record-keeping, self-monitoring and awareness that goals evolve over time. Through their interviews with children, SRL researchers identified what they called "self-evaluation" and "self-consequating" processes in which the children were actually living a desired goal in their imagination.

Seven Keys to Success Key 5 explains the process of setting goals. Key 6 provides two techniques that accelerate goal achievement through the development of creative imagination. Students learn that by Acting As If they are the person they want to be, they become more than they have ever been. The experience of success along the path to their goal accelerates motivation and progress toward achievement.

Summing up

Positive Psychology directs us to the path of personal success and achievement. The Seven Keys to Success Program builds a bridge across age, gender and socioeconomic challenges and provides the vehicle to carry us to our destination.

Adult role-modeling of positive attitude and positive habits is the best way to teach these essential life skills. Positive Psychology shares this perspective.

Psychological Foundations of The Seven Keys to Success

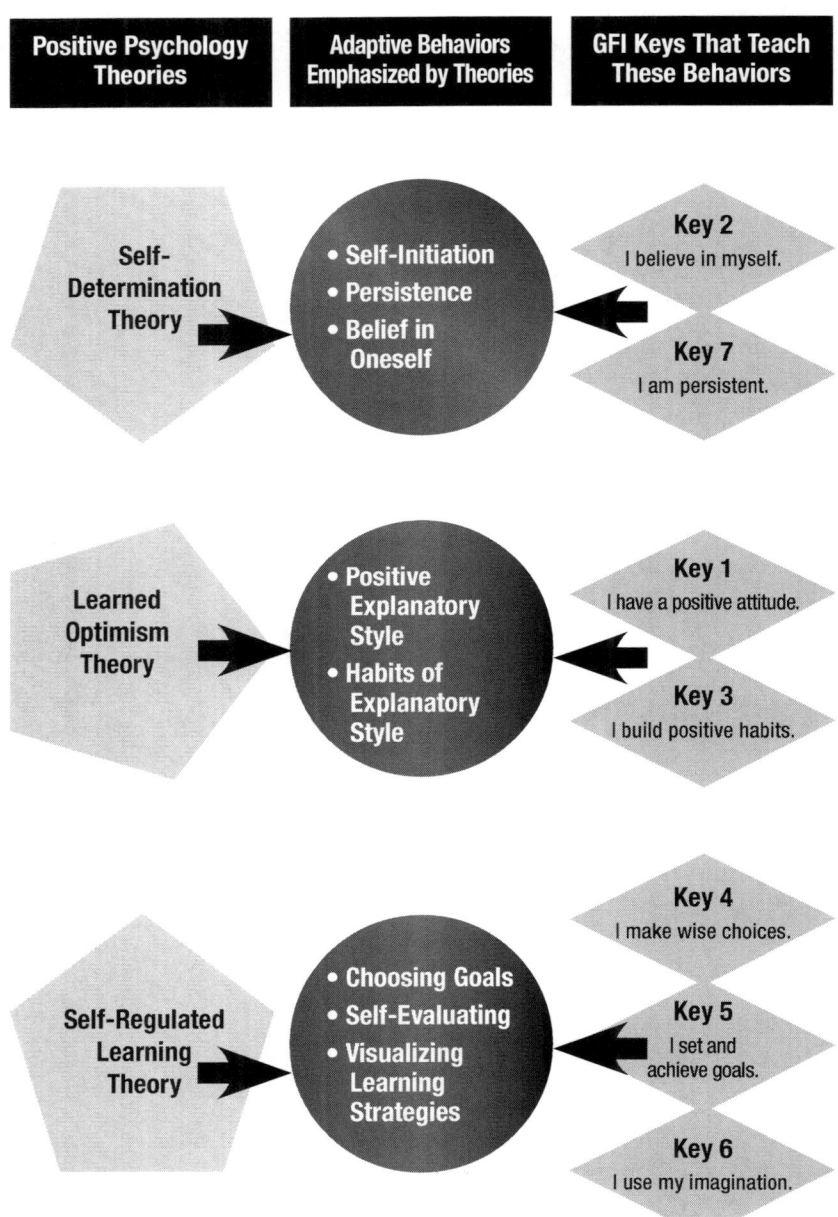

This figure shows how each of the Seven Keys to Success links to each of the three methodologies within the practice and theory of Positive Psychology. Although Positive Psychology and the Seven Keys to Success developed independently, they are tightly linked conceptually. The Seven Keys to Success Program clearly teaches strategies that researchers have identified as critical to success in and out of school. Source: "The Psychological Foundations of The Seven Keys to Success," Quality Evaluation Designs/QED, 2010.

For more detailed information about the Tombari & Lichtenstein research report, visit our website at www.goforitinstitute.org.

A Positive Attitude • Belief in One's Self • Positive Habits
Wise Choices • Setting and Achieving Goals
Using Creative Imagination • Persistence

IN CONCLUSION

An Invitation to You and Your Family to Become The Change We All Hope to Experience

In the Introduction, I acknowledged the challenges and frustrations we are facing and discussing across the country today. There is a feeling of restless energy as we talk about the future; we know something has to change.

In recent decades, when we've talked about what it would take to improve a particular condition in our country, we've spoken of the need for change in national and political terms. I believe we have come to a time when we understand that the changes needed to improve our lives and buttress the future of this country must come from within ourselves and our families.

> **There is a feeling of restless energy as we talk about the future; we know something has to change.**

The United States was born from the energy of a rebellion that gave birth to the greatest opportunity for freedom and achievement any nation has ever known. Can the energy of our present frustration give birth to a personal commitment to protect that freedom and opportunity for our families today?

I believe it can...and I believe you and your family have already taken a positive and powerful step in making this happen. One person, one family DOES make a difference. I invite you to consider the possibility of what your effort and example as individuals and as a family can do in terms of restoring hope and a real opportunity for everyone in this country.

Our country no longer leads educational achievement among the 30 developed nations of the world. Depending on the criteria used in the various assessment methods, the U.S. currently ranks between 25th and 27th. In the 1950s, the U.S. ranked within the top 3. Based on my nearly 3 decades of observation in our schools, I believe there is a way for our country to regain its educational achievement leadership and, in so doing, ensure a better future for everyone. I also believe this can be done inexpensively and quickly. Most important of all, I believe **you** and **your** family, along with **me** and **my** family, can be the catalyst for this transformation.

Here is what I know: Among nations where academic achieve-

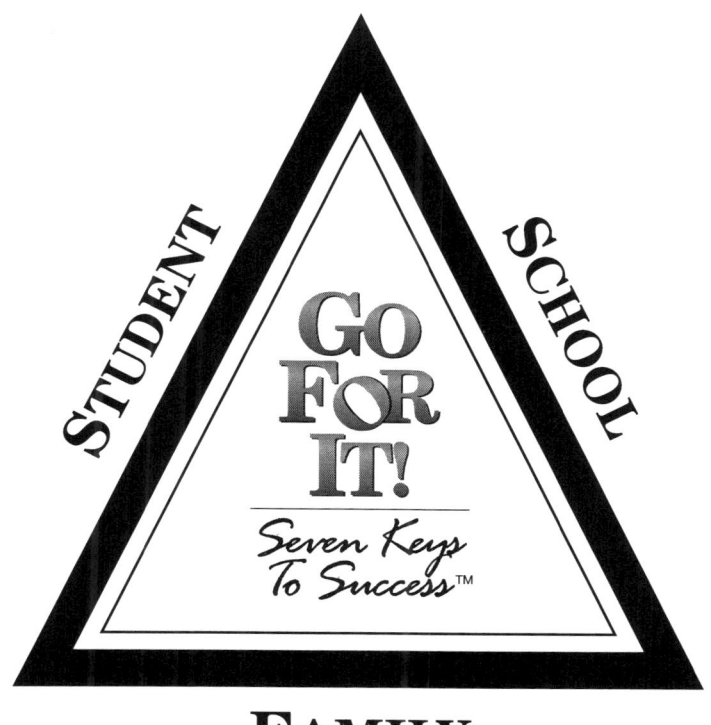

ment is high, there is a shared belief that educational achievement is fundamental to all aspects of social and economic success. The family, the student, and the school each takes an equilateral responsibility for a child's educational achievement. The responsibility for educating children is divided in this way:

- The family provides life skills, values' clarification and discipline.
- The student comes into the classroom motivated and prepared to learn.
- The school provides academic knowledge.

In the United States we have placed the responsibility for non-academic training (life skills, values' clarification and discipline) on our schools. K-12 classroom teachers tell us they are spending 20% to 60% of their teaching time on non-academic subjects such as life skills, values' clarification, and discipline. Over a period of several years, the National Institute for Student Motivation asked 10,000 teachers from the District of Columbia, Michigan, Illinois, Texas and California to identify the greatest need for achieving success in the classroom. An overwhelming preponderance of these educators ranked "students prepared to learn" at the top of the list. At the bottom of this list was: "increased funding."

With the school's shortened time for academic training and the students' lack of preparedness to learn, coupled with their resistance to work, even the best teachers in our country cannot provide superior academic education.

While the threats of war, terrorist attacks, environmental disasters and economic problems are a concern to all of us, our weakness in educational achievement is actually the greatest threat before us. Only a soundly educated population can successfully counter those other threats.

The good news is that we, as individuals and families, can turn this situation around.

Consider this: Social research tells us that a civilization advances when 10% of its population changes its thinking or behavior.

There are approximately 50,000,000 K-12 students in the United

States today. Of this population, 10% – 5,000,000 students – are members of 2,220,000 families.

What if 2,220,000 families took the responsibility for teaching their children life skills, providing values' clarification, and creating behavioral boundaries? The Seven Keys to Success embrace all of these! What if the 5,000,000 children in these families agreed to accept the responsibility for their own motivation and went to school each day prepared to learn and succeed?

> **When your success is added to the success of other families, it expands the hope that we can give our children a better tomorrow.**

Would you be willing to make a commitment to participate in this experiment with your family?

You have already invested $20 to purchase this book. An investment of one hour a week of your family time for six months in learning and practicing the skills of the Seven Keys – proven to work by people just like you – will provide you and your family with the knowledge and strategies to experience an easier and better life with greater opportunities for your future.

Your success with this experiment will undoubtedly bring a variety of rewards for you and your family. You will also be playing a significant role in education reform! When your success is added to the success of other families, it expands the hope that we can give our children a better tomorrow.

If 2,220,000 families make an investment of one hour a week for six months in working to increase their knowledge of what it takes to achieve and succeed – and regularly practice these strategies as a family team – we will experience positive change within our families, in the classrooms and in our country within one year.

If we want ourselves and our children to have a better future; if we want our country to be the leader it used to be... we CAN make this happen.
It's up to you and me.
Let's GO FOR IT!

ACKNOWLEDGEMENTS

The message of *Your Path To An EASIER & BETTER Life*
is connected to more people
than there are pages in this book.

I made a comment to my mother one day about how challenging it was to have three little children and how much I needed an escape. She sent me the money to buy an electric typewriter. I've often wondered if I'd have started writing without her gift. My mother believed in me. As did my father. My dad was the only person who never asked me if it was time to stop dreaming. I acknowledge the love, faith and continued support of my parents, Florence and Anthony Spinsky.

Your faith in the truth of this message is the glue that holds all the words on these pages.

The Seven Keys to Success were uncovered through interviews, set up by Helen Gray, Executive Director of the Horatio Alger Association, with 35 recipients of this organization's prestigious award for personal achievement. Among those outstanding men and women were William Dearden, W. Clement Stone and Dorothy L. Brown, MD; I will carry their stories with me forever.

I am probably the only person who realizes the importance of a phone call made to the Southland Corporation by Peter Brown of Traverse City, Michigan, creating the opportunity for that first school program in Texas. Pete, from your vantage point now, I hope you can see what your kindness set in motion. Thank you to Brenda Biederman and Sandy Shaw. The doors you opened led to the Verbal Hugs Radio Program and funding from Ronald McDonald's Children's Charities. You two were, in large part, the catalyst for all that happened after. Ken Barun, we never met in person, but your support played a significant role in the Go For It! Institute history.

Thank you to Dean Butler, Lauren Ward Larsen, Dr. Alton Takabayashi, Larry Del Santo and Denise Saddler, who created the opportunity for two years of developing the message in California … particularly in the Los Angeles Unified School District and Oakland Unified School District.

Thank you to all of you who attended our conferences, presentations and workshops over the years. Your responses and support reinforced my understanding of the importance of this work. Your faith in the truth of this message is the glue that holds all the words on these pages.

A special thank you to Steve and Michelle Wilson for providing the support to expand the opportunities of the GFI message. Your greatest gift, however, was your introduction of Mike Leikam. Mike, you re-energized the dream of bringing the GO FOR IT! message to classrooms and families everywhere. Your tireless effort, creativity, and belief in the importance of this work, gave me hope during a particularly challenging time in my life.

Sarah Mesmer, for me and GFI, the day we met was the equivalent of Neil Armstrong landing on the Moon. From where you stood, you could see forever and you gave us the vision that brought us to today. You are teacher, friend, angel, fellow-dreamer. Sandy Griffin, you made it possible for us to start GFI with your introduction to Sarah Bushong-Weeks. You also introduced us to Bill Schmidt…or as I lovingly call him, The Baffling Bannister. Bill, you have been my friend, my mentor and the image I see when I use the word integrity. Your faith, hard work and commitment to the idea of a better future for children has been the lifeblood of GFI. (You've also been the greatest source of cholesterol in our blood vessels with your gift of donuts at all our meetings over the years!)

Nila Tritt, Amy Matzen, Ellen Quest, you brought your wisdom and talent to our first GFI Board of Directors. Amy, you also brought Mary Anne Buczyna, our tireless, generous, determined first Executive Director, whose loving spirit will be a part of our organization forever.

John A. Warnick, I have been awed by your wisdom, intelligence and your ability to articulate the essence of God in all you communicate. Forrest Smith, I appreciate your enthusiasm for everything positive in the world. I am grateful for your friendship and commitment to making the world a better place.

Thank you, Liz Cady for joining the GFI board. You give your all to everything you do and I'm blessed to have you in my life. Thank you to Peggy Toal, Meshach Rhoades and Bernard Henriques for your contributions to our effort at the Institute.

The message of the Seven Keys to Success has been supported by the financial gifts of many who have become friends. At the top of that list are Bill Weeks and Sarah-Bushong Weeks, John and Mari Ann Martin, Nicole Hemsted and Susie McMurry.

The Institute is indebted to The Anschutz Foundation whose financial support sustained our organization and made the full development of our school program possible. I've been recipient to special effort put forth by a number of those in the Anschutz inner circle. Sarah and Chris Hunt, your visit to St. Rose of Lima in 2008, changed the history of the Institute, and allowed us to become who we are today. Libby Anschutz Brown, I'm indebted to you for making it possible for us to complete the family training component of our school program. Ted Harms, I respect and admire you more than anyone I've ever met. You are wise, brilliant, perceptive and kind. I'm grateful for the time and guidance you have so generously given me.

Thank you to the Daniels Fund. Your initial grant made it possible for us to turn the message of a workshop into a Master's in Education course for teachers. Someone who knew Bill Daniels well said his spirit was with us when we offered that first class for teachers and one of our students commented, "It should be against the law for anyone to teach without the knowledge of the GO FOR IT! Seven Keys to Success."

There have been many people who contributed significantly to moving the message of the Seven Keys to Success forward. Gregg Sherkin, Executive Director of Oprah Winfrey Foundation, John Arigoni and Tina Martinez, with Boys & Girls Clubs of Metro Denver, Christine Benero, CEO of Mile High United Way, Mark and Nancy

Bauman, Rutt and Annie Bridges all gave us significant help us along the way.

Marie, Ted and Mary, my wonderful children, your young lives provided the laboratory where the Seven Keys were tested and proven. Who you've become and what you've accomplished are testimony to the truth and power of the Keys. Chelsea, Arin, Zoe and Shane, my wonderful grandchildren, your parents' lives continue to be positive and powerful examples as you discover your own dreams and make them come true.

Thank you to my sisters, Mary Means and Donna Kuhar. You are my very best friends.

Teachers are my heroes. All of the work we do at the GO FOR IT! Institute is done in honor of teachers and those who work in our schools. I believe anyone who has ever achieved a dream has been encouraged and supported by the commitment and efforts of a teacher. I'm blessed to know some of the very best educators and support staff in our country. Among these are Jeannie Courchene, Geri Prager, Mary Sass, Kate Hardwick, Lucy Ontiveros, Barbara Bullock, Rick Grotzky, Karen Gogela, Sarah Rienecker, Veronica Benavidez, Loralie Cole, Joe and Cat DeRose.

Mari Stoll, Principal at Cottonwood Elementary School in the Natrona County School District of WY, and Cyndy Novotny, Principal of St. Anthony's Tri-Parish School in Casper, are two of the most exceptional people I've ever known. Mari and Cyndy are both educators and school administrators. Their insight and wisdom inspired our creation of a comprehensive curriculum for students in Pre-K through 8th grade as well as the development of our training component for parents and adults. Mari and Cyndy knew this comprehensive approach connecting schools, students and families had the potential for changing academic achievement anywhere. Their commitment to being instrumental in turning education around for all children was the catalyst for The CASPER Project, a five year study to determine the academic and personal achievement of students, fami-

> **You were the laboratory where the Seven Keys were tested!**
> **I'm proud of who you are and what you've accomplished.**

lies and educators. The CASPER Project is a collaboration of nine Natrona County Title I schools, the University of Wyoming Educational Leadership Department and the GO FOR IT! Institute. Data from Year One of this study already shows a dramatic decrease in behavior referrals as well as an equally impressive improvement in math and reading scores. Operational support for this study has been generously funded by a grant from the Bushong Family Foundation. In addition to Mari Stoll and Cyndy Novotny the other seven schools in this project are led by Principals Chris Carruth, Angie Hayes, Julie Hornby, Tammy Ray, Rene' Rickabaugh, Shawna Smith and Chris Tobin. The hard work and determined commitment of these nine principals in The CASPER Project will make history, along with the outstanding teachers and support staff in these schools in Natrona County, Wyoming: Bar Nunn Elementary, Cottonwood Elementary, Frontier Middle School, Midwest, Pineview Elementary, St. Anthony's Tri-Parish and University Park Elementary.

The parents, step-parents, grandparents, aunts/uncles other relatives and friends participating in The Casper Project are sharing stories of their own success in using the strategies of the Seven Keys to Success at home and in their jobs. They talk about what a difference it is making in their families. Casper families are proving they want to be part of the solution for helping students achieve and succeed to a higher degree than ever before. They are seeing for themselves that they have the power to be the greatest teachers in their children's lives. Casper families aren't just changing their children's lives; they are improving their own lives and lighting the way for families everywhere to do the same.

> **Teachers are my heroes. None of us can reach our potential or turn our dreams into reality without you.**

A special thanks to my dear friend, Krista Warnick for the blessed friendship we share. We are each other's cheerleaders.

Thank you to Debi Knight and Paulette Whitcomb, our designer and editor, for your years of diligent effort on our behalf. We've traveled through a lot of history together. I'm grateful for all your commitment and hard work.

And thank you, David McMurtry. I know you, above all, understand the importance of this work. I think our partnership in this dream has been part of a plan from the beginning... A beginning that may go further back than either of us knows.

My life has been enriched by the peaks and valleys along the journey of the Seven Keys. Thank you to everyone who touched my life along the way.

APPENDICES

APPENDIX A. Dictionary

- A -

ability *noun* 1. The quality of being able to do something; power: *Most people have the ability to dance.* 2. Power to do something, especially as the result of practice; skill: *You have a real ability as a dancer.*

accomplish *verb* To carry out: *We accomplished the job quickly.* Synonyms perform, accomplish, fulfill.

activity *noun* 1. Something done for fun: *Stamp collecting is my favorite activity.* 2. Energetic movement or action: *The store was a scene of great activity.*

attitude *noun* 1. A state of mind; a point of view: *Take a positive attitude toward studying.* 2. A position of the body showing a certain mood or condition.

attract *verb* 1. To draw to itself: A magnet attracts nails. 2. To draw by exciting interest or emotion: *They like to attract attention by wearing strange outfits.*

attraction *noun* The act or power of attracting.

automatic *adjective* 1. Capable of operating by or regulating itself. 2. Done without thought or control: *Breathing is an automatic function.*

- B -

belief *noun* 1. Confidence; trust: *We have a strong belief in justice for all.* 2. Something accepted as true.

benefit *noun* Something that is of help: *Eating properly is to your own benefit.*
verb 1. To be helpful or useful to. 2. To receive help of useful service: *I benefited from studying hard.*

- C -

characteristic *adjective* Showing a special feature or quality: typical: *The zebra has characteristic stripes.*
noun A special feature or quality: *Noise is a characteristic of most cities.*

choice *noun* 1. The act of choosing: *May I help you with your choice of books?* 2. The freedom or chance to choose. 3. Someone or something chosen: *Fish, a salad, and fruit were my choices for lunch.* 4. A variety from which to choose: *We had a wide choice of things to do after school.*
adjective worth being chosen above all others; excellent.
synonyms choice, alternative, preference, selection.

commit *verb* 1. To do; perform: *If you sew carelessly, you will commit errors.* 2. To put in confinement: *The criminal was committed to prison.* 3. To assign or devote to a certain course or activity; pledge: *We committed ourselves to helping others.*

confidence *noun* 1. A strong feeling of faith in oneself and one's ability: *I have confidence that I will win the race.* 2. Trust or faith in someone else or in something: *The coach has confidence in the team.*

conscious *adjective* 1. Able to see, feel and hear and to understand what is happening: *The patient is very ill but is still conscious.* 2. Able to know; aware: *Are you conscious of your own faults?* 3. Done with awareness: *Make a conscious effort to speak clearly.*

consciousness *noun* 1. the condition of being conscious: *The ill patient lost consciousness.* 2. All the thoughts, opinions, and feelings that a person or a group has.

consequence *noun* Something that happens as a result of another action or condition: *A consequence of cheating on this test will be suspension from school.*
synonyms effect, result.

- D -

develop *verb* 1. To make more effective or advanced: *Lessons will develop your musical ability.* 2. To grow or cause to grow: *Swimming develops the muscles.* 3. To bring or come into being: *Try to develop good reading habits.* 4. To treat a film with chemicals so that a picture can be seen.

development *noun* The act of developing or the condition of being developed.

discover *verb* 1. To find out; learn: *I looked down and discovered that my knee was bleeding.* 2. To be the first to find, learn of, or observe: *Who discovered the North Pole?*

discovery *noun* 1. The act of discovering. 2. Something discovered: *Penicillin was a great scientific discovery.*

- E -

energy *noun* The ability to act, work, or put forth mental or physical effort.

enjoyment *noun* 1. The act or condition of enjoying something: *One of the best things in life is the enjoyment of good food.* 2. A form or source of pleasure: *We work in the garden for enjoyment.*

enthusiasm *noun* A very strong, positive feeling for something; strong interest or admiration: *The children dive and swim with enthusiasm.*

experience *noun* 1. Something that one has taken part in or lived through: *The experience of being in an earthquake is never forgotten.* 2. Knowledge or skill gotten through practice: *You will need an education and experience to get a good job.*

experiential *adjective* Derived from, based on, or relating to experience: empirical.

- G -

generate *verb* To bring about or produce: *Water and steam generate electricity.*

goal *noun* 1. Something wanted or worked for; purpose. 2. The finish line of a race. 3. A structure or area into which players must drive a ball or puck in order to score in certain games. 4. A score awarded for driving a ball or puck into a goal.

good *adjective* 1. Having positive or desirable qualities: *Last week I read a good book.* 2. Suitable for a particular use: *Aluminum is a good material for pots and pans.* 3. Providing benefit; helpful: *Exercise is good for your health.* 4. Giving enjoyment; pleasant. 5. Better than the average. 6. Not weakened or damaged; sound. 7. Behaving properly: *Good children don't tell lies.* 8. Helpful and considerate; kind: *Be good to your parents and your friends.*
noun 1. Something that is good: *You have to accept the bad with the good.* 2. Something that is a benefit: *I'm doing this for your own good.*

- H -

habit *noun* 1. An activity or action done so often that one does it without thinking: *I have a habit of getting up early every morning.* 2. Clothing that is worn for a particular activity, such as horseback riding, or by membership of certain religious groups.

- I -

image *noun* 1. A picture of a real object formed by a lens, mirror, or other device: *When I looked through the telescope, the image was blurred.* 2. A picture in the mind of something that is not real or not present at the time. 3. A representation of a person or thing, such as a figure in a painting. 4. A person or thing that looks just like another: *I am the image of my cousin.*

imagination *noun* The act or power of forming a mental image of something not present to the senses or never before wholly perceived in reality.

interest *noun* 1. A feeling of wanting to give special attention to something: *The adventure book held my interest from the very first page.* 2. The quality of causing this feeling: *A boring movie lacks interest.* 3. Something that a person wants to give special attention to: *Music is one of my interests.* 4. Something that is to a person's advantage; benefit: *My parents always have my best interests at heart.* 5. A right, claim, or share in something: *Our parents wanted to buy an interest in the business.* 6. Money that is charged or paid for the use of borrowed money.

- K -

knowledge *noun* 1. Facts and ideas; information: *Listening in class is a good way to increase your general knowledge.* 2. Understanding; awareness: *The knowledge that the knife was sharp made me handle it carefully.*

- M -

magnetic *adjective* 1. Of or relating to magnetism or magnets. 2. Able to attract iron and steel. 3. Able to attract or fascinate other people.

mental *adjective* Of, relating to, or done in the mind: *Adding figures is a mental activity.*

- N -

negative *adjective* Lacking in positive qualities such as optimism and enthusiasm: *Your negative attitude is not helping you to make friends.*

notice *verb* To take note of; pay attention to: *I sat in the last row and hoped nobody would notice me.*

- O -

optimistic *adjective* Tending to take a hopeful or cheerful view of things.

- P -

passion *noun* 1. A powerful feeling, as love or hatred. 2. Great enthusiasm: *They have a passion for art.*

positive *adjective* Wanting to improve or develop; constructive: *If you have a positive attitude, you'll succeed.*

possible *adjective* 1. Capable of happening or being done: *It is possible to get to the airport by bus.* 2. Capable of being used for a certain purpose: *That field is a possible site for the new school.*

potential *noun* Something that can develop or become actual. *adjective* Possible but not yet actual, definite, or real: *People who look in store windows are potential customers.*

proactive *adjective* 1. Involving modification by a factor which precedes that which is modified. 2. Acting in anticipation of future problems, needs, or changes.

process *noun* A series of steps, actions, motions, or operations that bring about or lead to a result: *The farmer used a churn in the process of making butter.*

proof *noun* 1. Evidence of truth or accuracy: *We have no proof that the money was stolen.* 2. The act of a way of testing the quality or nature of something: *I put my beliefs to the proof.* 3. A test sheet of printed material to be checked for errors. 4. A test print of a photograph.

- R -

reaction *noun* A response to something: *I developed a rash as a reaction to the medicine.*

reactive *adjective* 1. Of, relating to, or marked by reaction or reactance. 2. Readily responsive to a stimulus. 3. Occurring as a result of stress of emotional upset: reactive depression.

result *noun* Something that happens because of something else: consequence: *All this damage is a result of the tornado.*
synonyms effect, consequence
verb 1. To come about as a result of something: *Floods resulted from the hurricane.* 2. To lead to a certain result: *Hard work results in success.*

Reticular Activating System *noun* The name given to the part of the brain (the reticular formation and its connections) believed to be the center of arousal and motivation in animals (including humans): *The activity of the Reticular Activating System is crucial for maintaining the state of consciousness.*

- S -

self-esteem *noun* A confidence and satisfaction in oneself: self-respect.

subconscious *noun* The mental activities just below the threshold of consciousness.

subject *noun* 1. One that is thought about, discussed, or represented. 2. A course or field of study: *Math is my favorite subject.* 3. One that is studied. 4. The word or group of words in a sentence that performs or receives the action of the verb. 5. A person under the authority, rule or control of another.

- T -

talent *noun* A natural ability to do something well: *If you give up music, you'll waste your talent.*

treasure *noun* 1. Wealth, such as jewels or money, that has been collected or hidden. 2. A very precious or valuable person or thing.

- V -

value *noun* 1. What something is worth in exchange for something else: *These shoes will give you good value for your money.* 2. The quality that makes something worth having; importance: *You should recognize the value of a good education.* 3. Estimated or determined worth: *The jeweler put a value of $9,000 on the diamond ring.*
verb 1. To believe to be of great worth or importance: I value your opinions. 2. To estimate or determine how much something is worth.

visualization *noun* 1. Formulation of mental visual images. 2. The act or process of interpreting in visual terms, or of putting into visible form.

- W -

wisdom *noun* Intelligence and good judgment in knowing what to do and being able to tell the difference between good and bad and right and wrong.

wise *adjective* Having or showing intelligence and good judgment: *A wise student studies for tests.*

wish *noun* 1. A strong desire for something: *My only wish is to be a teacher.* 2. An expression of a desire or hope: *We send you our best wishes for a happy birthday.*
verb 1. To long for; want: I wish you were here. 2. To have or express a wish for: *We wish you a safe trip.*

worth *noun* 1. The quality that makes someone or something expensive, valuable, useful, or important: *Your education will prove its worth.* 2. The amount that a certain sum of money will buy: *His father is worth over a million dollars.* 3. Deserving of: *The book is not worth reading.*

Sources

American Heritage Children's Dictionary. The Editors of American Heritage Dictionaries. New York: Houghton Mifflin Company, 1979,1994.

Merriam-Webster Online Dictionary. Springfield, Massachusetts: Merriam-Webster, Incorporated, 2005; www.m-w.com.

Webster's New Collegiate Dictionary. Springfield, Massachusetts: G. & C. Merriam Company, 1979.

Wikipedia. "Reticular Activating System." http://en.wikipedia.org/wiji/Reticular-activating_system.

APPENDICES

APPENDIX B. Habit Cards

A HABIT CARD is a simple, highly effective method for removing a negative, self-defeating image and replacing it with a positive, life-enhancing one.
The best way to prove this works is to try it!

Create Positive Habits:

1. **Identify the habit you want to change or create.**
2. **Write an effective HABIT CARD.**
   Write a very enthusiastic sentence for the habit you want to create, starting with:

   I, _____*(your name here)*_____ **,**

   Use one of these three words directly after your names:

   am, always, only

   Write your statement effectively using the 3 Ps:

   Personal, Positive, Present Tense

   _____*(name your goal)*_____

3. **Say your HABIT CARD out loud twice a day, with enthusiasm ... Watch your habits change!**

Reminder: Rewrite these statements on cards in your own handwriting.
This is a critical aspect of this technique.

I, _____(your name here)_____,
always keep my attitude POSITIVE! I always look for the good, make positive changes in myself or my situation, find a benefit or USE MY SMILE MAKER! I am a magnet for all the good my life can hold!

I, _____(your name here)_____,
am a Positive Person! I keep my focus on my gratitude for all that is good in my life!

I, _____(your name here)_____,
Believe in Myself! I am a life-long learner and a life-long doer!

I'm on a constant treasure hunt for subjects and activities I enjoy!

I, _____*(your name here)*_____,
am a better version of myself every day!
I learn something new or practice something I enjoy
each and every day! I bring good into the world by
learning more and participating more!

I, _____*(your name here)*_____,
teach other people how to believe in themselves by letting them see how I believe in me!
I am a student as well as a teacher!

I, _____*(your name here)*_____,
am a GREAT student! I listen in class.
I ask questions when I need help.
I do my homework. I am GREAT at taking tests!

I, _____(your name here)_____,
am a VERY healthy (man, woman, boy, girl)!
I ONLY eat foods that are healthy.
I only drink health-supporting drinks!
I glow with health from head to toe!

I, _____(your name here)_____,
only have health-supporting habits.
All my behaviors and activities support
the highest level of health!

I, _____(your name here)_____,
crave ONLY healthy food and drinks!
I am the poster child (or adult) for
Health and Well-Being!

I, _____(your name here)_____,

ALWAYS know before my day starts, how I want to feel at the end of the day. That makes all my choices during the day EASY! My positive choices make my life EASIER AND BETTER! I really am an awesome (man, woman, boy, girl)!

I, _____(your name here)_____,

ALWAYS choose wisely!
My wise choices guarantee the results I want!
I know personal power comes from wise choices!
My wise choices make me a winner every day!

I, _____(your name here)_____,

am a POWERFUL (man, woman, boy, girl) because I know the secret! I have the power to be the person I want to be through my wise choices!

> I, _____ *(your name here)* _____,
> have GOALS! I know it is always important to be
> working toward a clear goal. My goal for today is:
> _____. My Dream Goal for my life
> is: _____. I get to any goal with
> one step at a time!

> I, _____ *(your name here)* _____,
> can FEEL the happiness of working toward my goal of
> _____! I know I can achieve
> this goal because of how I feel whenever I think of
> achieving it!

> I, _____ *(your name here)* _____,
> know I have everything it takes to make my
> dream goal a reality! I know whatever I need to learn
> or do to reach my goal will come to me
> as it is needed along my journey to success!
> I WAS BORN TO ACHIEVE AND SUCCEED!

Appendix B. Habit Cards

I, _____*(your name here)*_____,
always remember the POWER of my Imagination! I take five minutes every day to go inside myself and "live" the feelings and experience of the achievement and celebration of reaching my goal! This five minutes is filled with joy and happiness!

I, _____*(your name here)*_____,
ALWAYS Act As If I am (describe the you that you want to be here). I know that Acting As If is the door that opens me to my Easier and Better life!

For Example: If your goal is to be loving and patient, your card might be worded like this: I, (your name here), ALWAYS Act As If I am loving and patient. I know this is how I am becoming the most loving and patient parent and human being in the world!

I, _____(your name here)_____,
am PERSISTENT! I never give up! I am unstoppable!
I just keep on taking one step toward my goal of
(name your goal) every day.
MY GOAL IS WORTH MY EFFORT!

I, _____(your name here)_____,
was born to achieve and succeed.
I am determined to achieve and succeed!
I am a winner because I AM Persistent!

I, _____(your name here)_____,
am proud to be a member of the (family name) team!
Our (family name) team makes a positive difference
in our school, (church name if applicable)
and neighborhood, state, and country!
We set a positive example for other families!

The examples of Habit Cards on the previous page are suggestions to help you create Habit Cards that will lead to the behaviors and mind set needed to replace any self-defeating behavior or mindset that may have previously caused challenges in your life. The best Habit Cards you can create for yourself are the ones you most want to see as the reality in your life.

Write your Habit Cards in the first person, present tense. Use to-the-point, positive and power-filled statements! Say them aloud a minimum of twice a day. Make sure you read your Habit Cards first thing in the morning and last thing at night. When you do say the words on your Habit Cards first thing in the morning and last thing at night, every day, week after week, those words WILL turn into your reality. To prove this works, all you have to do is follow these directions and you will see the results in your life and in the lives of those with whom you are doing this exercise. I know this works because I have experienced the transforming power of Habit Cards in my life for more than twenty years. I'm very happy to have the opportunity to share what I have learned with you! I encourage you to share this strategy with those you love and those you believe could benefit from it.

**Any self-defeating habit CAN be neutralized and replaced with a self-enhancing habit.
The more enthusiastically a HABIT CARD is read, the greater the number of weeks and months a HABIT CARD is read, the more powerful the new habit becomes.**

JUDY ZERAFA

Judy Zerafa is the founder of the GO FOR IT! Institute. She developed the Seven Keys to Success Life Program©, which is the basis of the education programs offered by the Institute, including a continuing education credit curriculum with a Masters in Education program. Zerafa is the author of *GO FOR IT!* (Workman Publishing/1982), the first self-help book for young people. *GO FOR IT!* was listed as a best-seller by Publisher's Weekly for seven years. Zerafa is an international speaker who has reached over 400 audiences including corporate executives and management teams, government agencies, civic and professional groups. Zerafa has also been extensively interviewed by media including *TODAY SHOW*, and *The Washington Post*.

Judy Zerafa's Seven Keys to Success Life Program was developed after extensive interviews with recipients of the Horatio Alger Award Recipients who have succeeded entirely through their own efforts; many of them despite adversity. Zerafa's research revealed seven specific principles these men and women believed were essential for all personal achievement and success. Zerafa realized these seven principles were exactly what all the writers and speakers on the subject of success had been teaching for decades. "Everyone was telling us WHAT we needed to know in order to succeed", said Zerafa. "What I realized was that no one was teaching anyone HOW to develop and use those seven principles!" The how-to part of achieving and succeeding in life was where Zerafa put her focus.

Your Path To An EASIER & BETTER Life is the step-by-step process anyone can use to achieve and succeed in school, relationships, jobs or careers…and in all life experiences. According to a White Paper published in 2010 by social researchers, Martin L. Tombari, Ph.D., and Gary Lichtenstein, Ed.D., the Seven Keys to Success developed by Zerafa ties the how-to strategies to the fundamental theories of Positive Psychology which is the universally accepted science of all Psychology practiced and taught today.

Judy Zerafa lives in Denver, CO. She is the mother of three, and grandmother of four

NOTES

To submit your own Seven Keys to Success Story
or to find out more information, please go to
www.EasierBetterLife.com or www.facebook.com/EasierBetterLife.

NOTES

To submit your own Seven Keys to Success Story
or to find out more information, please go to
www.EasierBetterLife.com or www.facebook.com/EasierBetterLife.

Made in the USA
San Bernardino, CA
16 March 2015